# CHAPTER-1

# INTRODUCTION TO INTRUSION PREVENTION SYSTEM

These days, the most of the organizations use signature-based intrusion detection along with CAPTCHA to detect intruders on their intranets. The fact behind this trend is that signature detection and CAPTCHA are well-known technologies, as compared to anomaly detection which is actively being researched. Along with this fact, anomalies based Intrusion Detection System are known to generate many alerts, where majority are false alarms. Therefore organizations need valuable comparisons between different tools in order to select which is best suited for their needs.

An Intrusion Prevention System (IPS) is a technology for network security or network threat prevention which examines the flow in network traffic in order to detect and prevent the vulnerability exploits.

Intrusion prevention systems which are also known as IDPS- Intrusion Detection and Prevention Systems are basically appliances for network security that monitor network or system activities or both for the purpose of malicious activities. The key functions of an Intrusion Prevention systems are to identify malicious activity, log information about this activity, attempt to either block or stop it and finally to report it for the purpose resolution.

Intrusion Prevention Systems are considered as extensions of Intrusion Detection Systems. The main differences are, unlike intrusion detection systems, intrusion prevention systems are placed in-line and are able to actively prevent/block intrusions that are detected. More specifically, IPS can take such actions as sending an alarm, dropping the malicious packets, resetting the connection and/or blocking the traffic from the offending IP address. An IPS can also correct Cyclic Redundancy Check (CRC) errors, unfragment packet streams, prevent TCP sequencing issues, and clean up unwanted transport and network layer options [NIST, 2007] .

1

We will see a different role of CAPTCHA in this book, CAPTCHA means that "Completely Automatic Public Turing test to tell Computers and Humans Apart". CAPTCHAs are used to prevent automatic registration of email accounts by spam bots and to prevent bulk mailing by the spammers. We will also discuss the tricks to fool users even if CAPTCHA is there in this book.

We would like to aim at finding a solution for intrusion detection methods in order to find out that which is best suited for Mission Critical Online Applications. An anomaly Intrusion Detection System needs to be trained, hence to establish the influence of the training period length of an anomaly Intrusion Detection System on its detection rate is another requirement.

In an article in Information Security titled "Mission: Critical", Stephen Barlas and others discuss cyber security and critical infrastructure. It will be a disaster if such Mission Critical system be attacked. Such consequences of a large scale and persistent outage of network applications can produce serious financial damage to a wide variety of companies.

A recent and famous example of a Network Intrusion is SKYPE -a registered trademark of SKYPE Limited in US and other Countries; which allows users to make Audio/Video telephone calls free of charge over the internet. This is basically a VoIP – Voice Over IP application working on Peer-to-Peer principle. It is using the existing infrastructure of Users and ISP - Internet Service Providers without any permission or user regulations or rather without any notification. This result in revenue loss, bandwidth loss for the users as well as ISP's and loss of processing power (CPU and memory) for the network hosts.

In present context we will consider "Application" as a software program, which is typically collection of computing operations embodied by certain set of instructions. The term "Intrusion" means an attempt to break into and / or misuse any computing system. The term "Intrusion Signature" means a communication pattern identified as corresponding to a new type of intrusion including patterns that may be found in individual packets and patterns that may be gleaned from analysing multiple packets.

2

If some abnormal communication behavior is detected, a process specific remedy is provided. E.g. Network communications for the process that has abnormal communication behavior may be terminated or monitored more closely. Additionally an alert of the detected intrusion may be sent to a system administrator. This alert may specifically identify the process, the computing system on which it is running and the type of abnormal behavior detected.

In the electronic communications medium Spamming is sending unsolicited and usually unwanted messages or emails in bulk without taking consent of the recipients. Email is one of the most common types of spam. Phishing is another and particular type of spam where a spammer attempts to masquerade in capacity of a reputed business. The objective is such spam mails is to retrieve sensitive information of recipients such as their bank account numbers, passwords, and credit card credentials. The Spam and phishing are causing losses to business usually in billions of dollars.

Many organizations are taking initiatives on different technical and legal levels for fighting this challenge. In this dissertation I have tried to examine these issues from different aspects such network protocols, human psychology, spammer psychology, working or zombies and spamming bots, spam filtering, scalability, etc.

We are going to study various problems with the present trending spam-fighting techniques. We will conclude that by using a combination of some spam-fighting techniques which are better than others. Following this we can create awareness with Internet users, different legal actions and cooperation of different entities within the industry, the spammers' business model can be disrupted in the next few years.

## 1.1 Network Intrusion Detection Systems

A network intrusion detection system (NIDS) has to be implemented just inside the application layer. Thus a network service requested by applications has to go to NIDS first, and NIDS should be having specific knowledge that which application is requesting which network service.

In information system, intrusions are the activities that violate the security policy of the system and process which identifies intrusions called Intrusion Detection. Around from last 20 years Intrusion detection has been studied. Basis for it was; an intruder's behavior will be noticeably different from that of a legitimate user and that many unauthorized actions will be detectable.

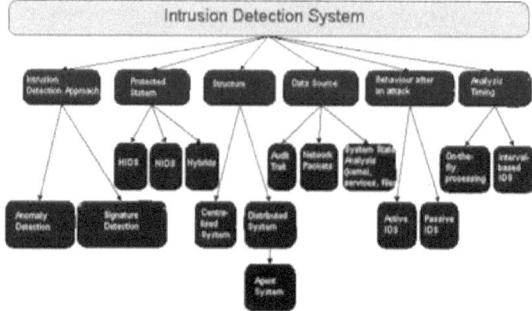

Figure 1: Classification of Intrusion Detection Systems

Whereas a firewall may be used in both home and commercial environments, Intrusion Detection Systems are only really feasible within commerce. They are generally expensive systems which are often termed "Intelligent Firewalls". The reason for this is that they utilize Artificial Intelligence techniques to monitor patterns in network activity. This monitoring process is conducted to detect spurious activity patterns. Figure 1 shows the recommended network integration for an intrusion detection system.

There are some important points that should be considered when integrating an IDS with a network. Initially, the IDS must capture and monitor all traffic within the network, not just that between itself and a switch. It is also necessary to place the IDS before the firewall in the network to get maximal detection of intrusion, as some intrusive packets may be filtered out by the firewall.

4

There are a number of reasons that make intrusion detection an essential part of the whole defence system. Initially, various traditional systems and applications were developed without taking security in mind. Later on, development of systems and applications were done to work in a diverse environment and may become vulnerable when deployed in the current environment. Main function of intrusion detection is to provide away to identify and thus allow responses to, attacks against these systems. Another reason is because of the limitations of information security and software engineering practice, computer systems and applications may have design flaws or bugs that could be used by an intruder to attack the systems or applications. As a result, certain preventive mechanisms (e.g., firewalls) may not be as effective as expected.

Intrusion detection improves the system security by complementing these protective mechanisms. In addition to, those preventive security mechanisms can protect information systems successfully, it is still desirable to know what intrusions have happened or are happening, so that we can understand the security threats and risks and thus be better prepared for future attacks.

Regardless of their importance, Intrusion detection systems are not replacements for preventive security mechanisms, such as access control and authentication. Certainly, Intrusion detection systems alone cannot provide enough security to information systems. Thus, Intrusion detection systems should be used along with other preventive security mechanisms as a part of a comprehensive defense system.

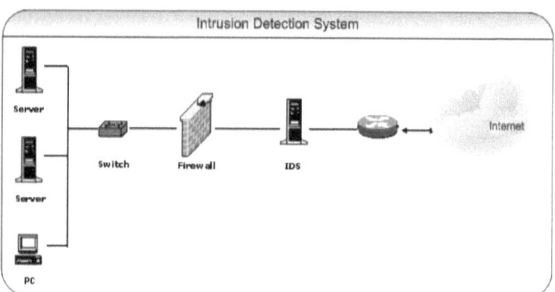

Figure 2: A Typical Intrusion Detection System

Conventionally intrusion detection techniques can be categorized into two methodologies:

- ❖ Anomaly based Intrusion Detection System
- ❖ Misuse detection based Intrusion Detection System

### 1.1.1 Anomaly based Intrusion Detection System

Anomaly based Intrusion Detection System is a system of detection of computer intrusions and the usage improper by the activity of the system of supervision and to classify it as normal or abnormal. The classification is based on heuristics or rules, rather than models or signatures, and stretched to detect any abuse type that falls of the normal functioning of the system. It is as opposed to the systems to signature basis that cannot detect the attacks for which ones a signature already was created.

Anomaly detection is based on the normal behavior of user or a system; any action that significantly deviates from the normal behavior is considered intrusive. Misuse detection catches intrusions in terms of the characteristics of known attacks or system vulnerabilities; any action that conforms to the pattern of a known attack or vulnerability is considered intrusive.

### 1.1.2 Misuse detection based Intrusion Detection System

Misuse detection based Intrusion Detection System is an approach in which we define abnormal system behaviour at first, and then define any other behaviour, as normal behaviour. It stands against anomaly detection approach which utilizes the reverse approach, defining normal system behaviour and defining any other behaviour as abnormal. In other words anything we don't know is normal. Using attack signatures in Intrusion Detection Systems is an example of this approach.

### 1.2 Intrusion Detection System Categories:

On the other hand, according to the sources of the audit information used by each Intrusion detection systems, Intrusion detection systems may be classified into following categories:

1. Host-based Intrusion detection systems

2. Distributed Intrusion detection systems

3. Network-based Intrusion detection systems

### 1.2.1 Host-based Intrusion Detection Systems (H-IDS)

A Host based Intrusion Detection System, (H-IDS) on the host oversees the entirety or on the part dynamic behaviour and the computer state of a system. Besides these activities as the dynamic inspection of the packages network intend for this specific host (component in option with most of the solutions logicielles available in the commerce), an H-IDS can detect which program attains which resources and to discover that, for example, a word processing suddenly has and inexplicably begun modifying the basis of data password system. Of even a H-IDS could resemble the state system, information is stocked, that it is in RAM, in the file system, the files newspapers or elsewhere, and verify that the content of these appear as foreseen, for e.g. not modified by intruder.

Host-based Intrusion detection systems get audit data from host audit trails and usually aim at detecting attacks against a single host; distributed IDS's gather audit data from multiple hosts and possibly the network that connects the hosts, aiming at detecting attacks involving multiple hosts. Network-based Intrusion detection systems use network traffic as the audit data source, relieving the burden on the hosts that usually provide normal computing services.

### 1.2.2 Distributed Intrusion Detection Systems (D-IDS)

A distributed IDS (D-IDS) is composed of several systems of detection of Intrusion Detection Systems on a big network, that all communiqués between them, or with a central waiter that facilitates the supervision of the network of not at all, the analysis of the incidents and data of instantaneous attack. In having these cooperative distributed agents through a network, the incident analysts, the operations network and of security of the personnel are in a position to obtain a wider vision of what happens on their network in his body.

A D-IDS allows equally to a business to manage efficiently its resources of analysis of the incidents while centralizing its files of attack and while giving to the analyst a quick and easy means to spot the new tendencies and characteristic and to identify the threats that weigh on the network through several segments of network. This item will discuss the distributed systems of detection of intrusion, including the general configuration of a D-IDS and a study of fictitious case to show the capacities of distributed analysis. She will attempt equally to give to the reader a summary of the advantages of the management of a system of D-IDS, analyst of the incident and the two views of business.

### 1.2.3 Network-based Intrusion detection systems (N-IDS)

A system of detection of intrusion of network is most often to place strategic points in a network, so as to be able to oversee the traffic destination or in origin of the different devices of this network. While choosing such a system, you must compare the principal types of a system of detection of intrusion network. There exist two such types of systems on this principle. A system based on the signature and the other is a based system on an

8

abnormality. A system based on the signature of detection of intrusion is granted to a special vulnerability, it has therefore less the number of positive false one (FP), while the system will look for an abnormality bases for attacks that are outside the norms, which will increase the rate of positive false one. Consequently, you must choose a system according to your specific needs.

### 1.3 Functions of an Intrusion Detection System:

An IDS- Intrusion Detection System is usually designed in order to monitor all inbound and outbound network activities and identify any suspicious patterns that may indicate a network or system attack from someone attempting to break into or compromise a system. IDS is considered to be a passive-monitoring system, since the main function of an IDS product is to warn you of suspicious activity taking place and not to prevent them. An IDS essentially reviews your network traffic and data and will identify probes, attacks, exploits and other vulnerabilities. IDSs can respond to the suspicious event in one of several ways, which includes displaying an alert, logging the event or even paging an administrator. In some cases the IDS may be prompted to reconfigure the network to reduce the effects of the suspicious intrusion .

An IDS specifically looks for suspicious activities and events that might be the result of a virus, worm or hacker. This is done by looking for known intrusion signatures or attack signatures that characterize different worms or viruses and by tracking general variances which differ from regular system activity. The IDS is able to provide notification of only known attacks.

The term IDS actually covers a large variety of products, for which all produce the end result of detecting intrusions. An IDS solution can come in the form of cheaper shareware or freely distributed open source programs, to a much more expensive and secure vendor software solution. Additionally, some IDSs consist of both software applications and hardware appliances and sensor devices which are installed at different points along your network.

**There are several ways to categorize an IDS system:**

**a) Misuse Detection vs. Anomaly Detection**

In misuse detection, the IDS analyzes the information it gathers and compares it to large databases of attack signatures. Essentially, the IDS looks for a specific attack that has already been documented. Like a virus detection system, detection software is only as good as the database of intrusion signatures that it uses to compare packets against. In anomaly detection, the system administrator defines the baseline, or normal, state of the network's traffic load, breakdown, protocol, and typical packet size. The anomaly detector monitors network segments to compare their state to the normal baseline and look for anomalies.

**b) Passive Vs. Reactive Systems**

In a passive system, the IDS detects' a potential security breach, logs the information and signals an alert. In a reactive system, the IDS respond to the suspicious activity by logging off a user or by reprogramming the firewall to block network traffic from the suspected malicious source.

**c) Network-based vs. Host-based IDS**

Intrusion detection systems are network or host based solutions. Network-based IDS systems (NIDS) are often standalone hardware appliances that include network intrusion detection capabilities. It will usually consist of hardware sensors located at various points along the network or software that is installed to system computers connected to your network, which analyzes data packets entering and leaving the network. Host-based IDS systems (HIDS) do not offer true real-time detection, but if configured correctly are close to true real-time.

Host-based IDS systems consist of software agents installed on individual computers within the system. HIDS analyze the traffic to and from the specific computer on which the intrusion detection software is installed on. HIDS systems often provide features you can't get with a network-based IDS. For example, HIDS are able to monitor activities that only an administrator should be able to implement. It is also able to monitor changes to key system files and any attempt to overwrite these files. Attempts to install Trojans or backdoors can also be monitored by a HIDS and stopped. These specific intrusion events are not always seen by a NIDS.

While it depends on the size of your network and the number of individual computers which require intrusion detection system, NIDS are usually a cheaper solution to implement and it requires less administration and training – but it is not as versatile as a HID. Both systems will require Internet access (bandwidth) to ensure they system is kept up-to-date with the latest virus and worm signatures.

**The main functions of a network intrusion detection system include:**

- ❖ **Detecting attacks:** such a system detects security threats and attacks as and when they happen by providing real-time network monitoring.
- ❖ **Offer information:** If this system detects an attack, then it put forward information about the attack.
- ❖ **Take corrective steps:** Once an attack is detected by the system, the active systems also take measure to tackle the attack.
- ❖ **Storage:** It also stores the events either locally or otherwise in case of an attack.

With use of these functions an effective Intrusion Detection System can be made.


### 1.4 TCP/IP Protocol and Intrusion System

The protocol that Internet and many of today's networks based on-Transmission Control Protocol and Internet protocol (TCP/IP), was first developed in 1979. The primary focus was to ensure reliable communications between groups of networks connected by computers acting as gateways. At that time, security was not a primary concern due to the size of this Internet and that most of the users were familiar to each other. However, the base technologies used to construct this network contained many insecurities, most of which still exist today. Due to a number of well reported attacks on private networks originating from the Internet, security has become a primary

11

concern for organizations connecting to the Internet. Organizations need to securely conduct business and protect their data and computing from attacks. Such needs are heightened as businesses link geographically distant parts of the organization using private networks based on TCP/IP as stated by Oliver et.al .

Intrusion prevention presents its own difficulties. Intrusion prevention systems (IPS's), mostly, prevent attacks that fit an established pattern or "signature." This leaves the network vulnerable to new, undocumented attack strategies. IPS's also tend to yield a large number of false positives – thereby wasting staff time and eventually causing a real attack to be ignored. Other types of anomaly recognition systems are similarly prone to generating false positives, since they trigger alerts whether a deviation has an innocuous or a malicious cause. Finally, intrusion prevention and anomaly systems are reactive; the action against an attack is taken as it occurs by resetting TCP connections or requesting a firewall rule change, which are mostly not fast enough to prevent the attack.

### 1.5 Intrusion Prevention Principles

Intrusion prevention is a preemptive approach to network security used to identify potential threats and respond to them swiftly. However, because an exploit may be carried out very quickly after the attacker gains access, intrusion prevention systems also have the ability to take immediate action, based on a set of rules established by the network administrator. For example, an IPS might drop a packet that it determines to be malicious and block all further traffic from that IP address or port. Legitimate traffic, meanwhile, should be forwarded to the recipient with no apparent disruption or delay of service.

According to Michael Reed of Top Layer Networks, an effective intrusion prevention system should also perform more complex monitoring and analysis, such as watching and responding to traffic patterns as well as individual packets. "Detection mechanisms can include address matching, HTTP string and substring matching, generic pattern matching, TCP connection analysis, packet anomaly detection, traffic anomaly detection and TCP/UDP port matching."Intrusion prevention is the process of monitoring the events occurring in a computer system or network and analyzing them for signs of possible incidents, which are violations or imminent threats of violation of computer security policies, acceptable use policies, or standard security practices. Incidents have many causes, such as malware (e.g., worms, spyware), attackers gaining unauthorized access to systems from the Internet, and authorized users of systems who misuse their privileges or attempt to gain additional privileges for which they are not authorized. Although many incidents are malicious in nature, many others are not; for example, a person might mistype the address of a computer and accidentally attempt to connect to a different system without authorization.

An intrusion prevention system (IPS) is software that has all the capabilities of an intrusion detection system and can also attempt to stop possible incidents. This section provides an overview of IPS technologies as a foundation for the rest of the thesis. It first explains how IPS technologies can be used. Next, it describes the key functions that IPS technologies perform and the detection methodologies that they use. Finally, it provides an overview of the major classes of IPS technologies.

**Intrusion Prevention Systems are using following key principles :**
1. Durability or Reliability of Prevention System;
2. Minimal Reports of False Positives;
3. Maximum Intrusion Detection capabilities;
4. Minimal Maintenance of this system;
5. Ability to accurately find out the Intrusion attack location;
6. Ability to integrate or incorporate with other complementary technologies.

### 1.6  Uses of Intrusion Prevention System Technologies

Intrusion Prevention System (IPS) is primarily focused on identifying possible incidents. If the IPS had successfully prevented the attack, security administrators still might want to be notified of the attack. This is particularly important if the target has a known vulnerability that the attack could have exploited. Attackers could potentially use a different attack for the same vulnerability that the IPS might not recognize.

The IPS could also log information that could be used by the incident handlers [NIST  ]. Many IPS's can also be configured to recognize violations of security policies. Many IPS's can also identify reconnaissance activity, which may indicate that an attack is imminent. For example, some attack tools and forms of malware, particularly worms, perform reconnaissance activities such as host and port scans to identify targets for subsequent attacks.

In addition to identifying incidents and supporting incident response efforts, organizations have found other uses for IPS's, including the following:

a) Identifying security policy problems. An IPS can provide some degree of quality control for security policy implementation, such as duplicating firewall rule sets and alerting when it sees network traffic that should have been blocked by the firewall but was not because of a firewall configuration error.

b) Documenting the existing threat to an organization. IPS's log information about the threats that they detect. Understanding the frequency and characteristics of attacks against an organization's computing resources is helpful in identifying the appropriate security measures for protecting the resources. The information can also be used to educate management about the threats that the organization faces.

c) Deterring individuals from violating security policies. If individuals are aware that their actions are being monitored by IPS technologies for security policy violations, they may be less likely to commit such violations because of the risk of detection.

Because of the increasing dependence on information systems and the prevalence and potential impact of intrusions against those systems, IPS's have become a necessary addition to the security infrastructure of nearly every organization.

## 1.7 Summary

Intrusion prevention is the process of monitoring the events occurring in a computer system or network and analyzing them for signs of possible incidents, which are violations or imminent threats of violation of computer security policies, acceptable use policies, or standard security practices. Intrusion prevention is also the process of performing intrusion detection and attempting to stop detected possible incidents. Intrusion prevention systems (IPS) are primarily focused on identifying possible incidents, logging information about them, attempting to stop them, and reporting them to security administrators. In addition, organizations use IPS's for other purposes, such as identifying problems with security policies, documenting existing threats, and deterring individuals from violating security policies. IPS's have become a necessary addition to the security infrastructure of nearly every organization.

IPS's typically record information related to observed events, notify security administrators of important observed events, and produce reports. Many IPS's can also respond to a detected threat by attempting to prevent it from succeeding. They use several response techniques, which involve the IPS stopping the attack itself, changing the security environment (e.g., reconfiguring a firewall), or changing the attack's content.

IPS's cannot provide completely accurate detection; they all generate false positives (incorrectly identifying benign activity as malicious) and false negatives (failing to identify malicious activity). Many organizations choose to tune IDPS's so that false negatives are decreased and false positives increased, which necessitates additional analysis resources to differentiate false positives from true malicious events. Most IDPS's also offer features that compensate for the use of common evasion techniques, which modify the format or timing of malicious activity to alter its appearance but not its effect, to attempt to avoid detection by IPS's.

### Chapter Reference:

1. "NIST – Guide to Intrusion Detection and Prevention Systems (IDPS)" (PDF). February 2007.

2. S. Barlas, A. Earls, M. Fitzgerald, J. Ledford, D. McCafferty, "Mission: Critical", Information Security, September 2004 pg. 26.

3. "Free Skype internet calls", www.skype.com

SKYPE- Wikipedia, *http://en.wikipedia.org/wiki/Skype*

4. "Internet Security", *http://www.ukessays.com/essays/computer-science/ internet-security.php*

5. A typical Intrusion Detection System,

*www.cs.bham.ac.uk/~mdr/teaching/modules03/security/students/SS1/hando ut/handout.html*

6. *http://www.webopedia.com/DidYouKnow/Computer_Science/intrusion_ detection_prevention.asp*

7. Oliver J., Leahy Dermot M., Tynan J., Mark Smith, Sean G. Doherty, "Firewall technology", Digital Technical Journal, (2),1997.

8. NIST Special Publication (SP) 800-61, Computer Security Incident Handling Guide, *http://csrc.nist.gov/publications/nistpubs/*

# CHAPTER – 02

# INTRUSION DETECTION SYSTEM⬚

# (BACKGROUND AND OVERVIEW)

## 2.1 Network Intrusion Detection Systems

A network intrusion detection system (NIDS) has to be implemented just inside the application layer. Thus a network service requested by applications has to go to NIDS first, and NIDS should be having specific knowledge that which application is requesting which network service.

Conventionally intrusion detection techniques can be categorized into two methodologies:

- ❖ Anomaly based Intrusion Detection System
- ❖ Misuse detection based Intrusion Detection System

**2.1.1 Anomaly based Intrusion Detection System,** is a system of detection of computer intrusions and the usage improper by the activity of the system of supervision and to classify it as normal or abnormal. The classification is based on heuristics or rules, rather than models or signatures, and stretched to detect any abuse type that falls of the normal functioning of the system. It is as opposed to the systems to signature basis that cannot detect the attacks for which ones a signature already was created.

Anomaly detection is based on the normal behavior of user or a system; any action that significantly deviates from the normal behavior is considered intrusive. Misuse detection catches intrusions in terms of the characteristics of known attacks or system vulnerabilities; any action that conforms to the pattern of a known attack or vulnerability is considered intrusive.

**2.1.2 Misuse detection based Intrusion Detection System,** is an approach in which we define abnormal system behaviour at first, and then define any other behaviour, as normal behaviour. It stands against anomaly detection approach which utilizes the reverse approach, defining normal system behaviour and defining any other behaviour as abnormal. In other words anything we don't know is normal. Using attack signatures in Intrusion Detection Systems is an example of this approach.

## 2.2 Intrusion Detection System Categories:

On the other hand, according to the sources of the audit information used by each Intrusion detection systems, Intrusion detection systems may be classified into following categories:

- ❖ Host-based Intrusion detection systems
- ❖ Distributed Intrusion detection systems
- ❖ Network-based Intrusion detection systems

### 2.2.1 Host-based Intrusion detection Systems (H-IDS)

A Host based Intrusion Detection System, (H-IDS) on the host oversees the entirety or on the part dynamic behavior and the computer state of a system. Besides these activities as the dynamic inspection of the packages network intend for this specific host (component in option with most of the solutions logically available in the commerce), a H-IDS can detect which program attains which resources and to discover that.

Host-based Intrusion detection systems get audit data from host audit trails and usually aim at detecting attacks against a single host; distributed IDS's gather audit data from multiple hosts and possibly the network that connects the hosts, aiming at detecting attacks involving multiple hosts. Network-based Intrusion detection systems use network traffic as the audit data source, relieving the burden on the hosts that usually provide normal computing services.

### 2.2.2 Distributed Intrusion detection systems (D-IDS)

A distributed IDS (D-IDS) is composed of several systems of detection of Intrusion Detection Systems on a big network, that all communicates among them, or with a central service that facilitates the supervision of the network of not at all, the analysis of the incidents and data of instantaneous attack. In having these cooperative distributed agents through a network, the incident analysts, and the operations network and of security of the personnel are in a position to obtain a wider vision of what happens on their network in his body.

A D-IDS allows equally to a business to manage efficiently its resources of analysis of the incidents while centralizing its files of attack and while giving to the analyst a quick and easy means to spot the new tendencies and characteristic and to identify the threats that weigh on the network through several segments of network.

### 2.2.3 Network-based Intrusion detection systems (N-IDS)

A system of detection of intrusion of network is most often to place strategic points in a network, so as to be able to oversee the traffic destination or in origin of the different devices of this network. While choosing such a system, you must compare the principal types of a system of detection of intrusion network. There exist two such types of systems on this principle. A system based on the signature and the other is a based system on an abnormality. A system based on the signature of detection of intrusion is granted to a special vulnerability, it has therefore less the number of positive false one (FP), while the system will look for an abnormality bases for attacks that are outside the norms, which will increase the rate of positive false one. Consequently, you must choose a system according to your specific needs.

### 2.3 Intrusion Prevention Principles

Intrusion prevention is the process of monitoring the events occurring in a computer system or network and analyzing them for signs of possible incidents, which are violations or imminent threats of violation of computer security policies, acceptable use policies, or standard security practices. Incidents have many causes, such as malware (e.g., worms, spyware), attackers gaining unauthorized access to systems from the Internet, and authorized users of systems who misuse their privileges or attempt to gain additional privileges for which they are not authorized. Although many incidents are malicious in nature, many others are not; for example, a person might mistype the address of a computer and accidentally attempt to connect to a different system without authorization.

### 2.3.1 Key Functions of IPS Technologies

There are many types of IPS technologies, which are differentiated primarily by the types of events that they can recognize and the methodologies that they use to identify incidents. In addition to monitoring and analyzing events to identify undesirable activity, all types of IPS technologies typically perform the following functions:

A. Recording information related to observed events. Information is usually recorded locally, and might also be sent to separate systems such as centralized logging servers, security information and event management (SIEM) solutions, and enterprise management systems.

B. Notifying security administrators of important observed events. This notification, known as an alert, occurs through any of several methods, including the following: e-mails, pages, messages on the IDPS user interface, Simple Network Management Protocol (SNMP) traps, syslog messages, and user-defined programs and scripts. A notification message typically includes only basic information regarding an event; administrators need to access the IDPS for additional information.

C. Producing reports. Reports summarize the monitored events or provide details on particular events of interest.

Some IPS's are also able to change their security profile when a new threat is detected. For example, an IPS might be able to collect more detailed information for a particular session after malicious activity is detected within that session. An IPS might also alter the settings for when certain alerts are triggered or what priority should be assigned to subsequent alerts after a particular threat is detected.

**IDP's use several response techniques, which can be divided into the following groups:**

The IPS stops the attack itself. Examples of how this could be done are as follows:

❖ Terminate the network connection or user session that is being used for the attack

❖ Block access to the target (or possibly other likely targets) from the offending user account, IP address, or other attacker attribute

❖ Block all access to the targeted host, service, application, or other resource.

The IPS changes the security environment. The IPS could change the configuration of other security controls to disrupt an attack. Common examples are reconfiguring a network device (e.g., firewall, router, switch) to block access from the attacker or to the target, and altering a host-based firewall on a target to block incoming attacks. Some IPSs can even cause patches to be applied to a host if the IPS detects that the host has vulnerabilities.

The IPS changes the attack's content. Some IPS technologies can remove or replace malicious portions of an attack to make it benign. A simple example is an IPS removing an infected file attachment from an e-mail and then permitting the cleaned email to reach its recipient. A more complex example is an IPS that acts as a proxy and normalizes incoming requests, which means that the proxy repackages the payloads of the requests, discarding header information. This might cause certain attacks to be discarded as part of the normalization process.

Another common attribute of IPS technologies is that they cannot provide completely accurate detection. When an IPS incorrectly identifies benign activity as being malicious, a false positive has occurred. When an IPS fails to identify malicious activity, a false negative has occurred. It is not possible to eliminate all false positives and negatives; in most cases, reducing the occurrences of one increases the occurrences of the other. Many organizations choose to decrease false negatives at the cost of increasing false positives, which means that more malicious events are detected but more analysis resources are needed to differentiate false positives from true malicious events. Altering the configuration of an IPS to improve its detection accuracy is known as tuning.

## 2.4 Common Intrusion Detection Methodologies used in IPS

IPS technologies use many methodologies to detect incidents. The primary classes of detection methodologies are: signature-based, anomaly-based, and stateful protocol analysis, respectively. Most IPS technologies use multiple detection methodologies, either separately or integrated, to provide more broad and accurate detection.

### 2.4.1 Signature-Based Detection

A signature is a pattern that corresponds to a known threat. Signature-based detection is the process of comparing signatures against observed events to identify possible incidents. Examples of signatures are as follows:

❖ A telnet attempt with a username of "root", which is a violation of an organization's security policy
❖ An e-mail with a subject of "Free Hot Pictures!" and an attachment filename of "hotpics.exe", which are characteristics of a known form of malware
❖ An operating system log entry with a status code value of 645, which indicates that the host's auditing has been disabled.

Signature-based detection is very effective at detecting known threats but largely ineffective at detecting previously unknown threats, threats disguised by the use of evasion techniques, and many variants of known threats. For example, if an attacker modified the malware in the previous example to use a filename of "hotpics2.exe", a signature looking for "hotpics.exe" would not match it.

Signature-based detection is the simplest detection method because it just compares the current unit of activity, such as a packet or a log entry, to a list of signatures using string comparison operations. Signature-based detection technologies have little understanding of many network or

22

application protocols and cannot track and understand the state of complex communications. For example, they cannot pair a request with the corresponding response, such as knowing that a request to a Web server for a particular page generated a response status code of 403, meaning that the server refused to fill the request. They also lack the ability to remember previous requests when processing the current request. This limitation prevents signature-based detection methods from detecting attacks that comprise multiple events if none of the events contains a clear indication of an attack.

### 2.4.2 Anomaly-Based Detection

Anomaly-based detection is the process of comparing definitions of what activity is considered normal against observed events to identify significant deviations. An IPS using anomaly-based detection has profiles that represent the normal behaviour of such things as users, hosts, network connections, or applications. The profiles are developed by monitoring the characteristics of typical activity over a period of time. For example, a profile for a network might show that Web activity comprises an average of 13% of network bandwidth at the Internet border during typical workday hours. The IPS then uses statistical methods to compare the characteristics of current activity to thresholds related to the profile, such as detecting when Web activity comprises significantly more bandwidth than expected and alerting an administrator of the anomaly. Profiles can be developed for many behavioural attributes, such as the number of e-mails sent by a user, the number of failed login attempts for a host, and the level of processor usage for a host in a given period of time.

The major benefit of anomaly-based detection methods is that they can be very effective at detecting previously unknown threats. For example, suppose that a computer becomes infected with a new type of malware. The malware could consume the computer's processing resources, send large numbers of e-mails, initiate large numbers of network connections, and perform other behaviour that would be significantly different from the established profiles for the computer.

An initial profile is generated over a period of time (typically days, sometimes weeks) sometimes called a training period. Profiles for anomaly-based detection can either be static or dynamic. Once generated, a static profile is unchanged unless the IPS is specifically directed to generate a new profile. A dynamic profile is adjusted constantly as additional events are observed. Because systems and networks change over time, the corresponding measures of normal behaviour also change; a static profile will eventually become inaccurate, so it needs to be regenerated periodically. Dynamic profiles do not have this problem, but they are susceptible to evasion attempts from attackers. For example, an attacker can perform small amounts of malicious activity occasionally and then slowly increase the frequency and quantity of activity. If the rate of change is sufficiently slow, the IPS might think the malicious activity is normal behaviour and include it in its profile. Malicious activity might also be observed by an IPS while it builds its initial profiles.

Inadvertently including malicious activity as part of a profile is a common problem with anomaly-based IPS products. (In some cases, administrators can modify the profile to exclude activity in the profile that is known to be malicious.) Another problem with building profiles is that it can be very challenging in some cases to make them accurate, because computing activity can be so complex. For example, if a particular maintenance activity that performs large file transfers occurs only once a month, it might not be observed during the training period; when the maintenance occurs, it is likely to be considered a significant deviation from the profile and trigger an alert. Anomaly-based IPS products often produce many false positives because of benign activity that deviates significantly from profiles, especially in more diverse or dynamic environments. Another noteworthy problem with the use of anomaly-based detection techniques is that it is often difficult for analysts to determine why a particular alert was generated and to validate that an alert is accurate and not a false positive, because of the complexity of events and number of events that may have caused the alert to be generated.

### 2.4.3 Stateful Protocol Analysis

Stateful protocol analysis is the process of comparing predetermined profiles of generally accepted definitions of benign protocol activity for each protocol state against observed events to identify deviations. Unlike anomaly-based detection, which uses host or network-specific profiles, stateful protocol analysis relies on vendor-developed universal profiles that specify how particular protocols should and should not be used. The "stateful" in stateful protocol analysis means that the IDPS is capable of understanding and tracking the state of network, transport, and application protocols that have a notion of state. For example, when a user starts a File Transfer Protocol (FTP) session, the session is initially in the unauthenticated state. Unauthenticated users should only perform a few commands in this state, such as viewing help information or providing usernames and passwords. An important part of understanding state is pairing requests with responses, so when an FTP authentication attempt occurs, the IDPS can determine if it was successful by finding the status code in the corresponding response. Once the user has authenticated successfully, the session is in the authenticated state, and users are expected to perform any of several dozen commands. Performing most of these commands while in the unauthenticated state would be considered suspicious, but in the authenticated state performing most of them is considered benign.

### 2.5 Phases of attacks

It is not an easy task to provide security and prevent attacks. In order to protect digital information and other network assets, thinking methodology and behavior of the attacker can help to find out a way to prevent them. A professional attacker will thoroughly investigate the target systems, and ensure that everything is safe for the attack without being detected. Then they attack in a very structured manner while consistently monitoring the effect. This type of attacker threat tends to be far more thorough than the hobbyist or novice attacker who generally downloads ready-made exploitation scripts as they become available. Due to this thoroughness, attackers have a much higher success rate and do not usually get caught in the act. To properly assess the security of a system, an understanding of the different phases of a successful attack or intrusion is necessary. By understanding the risk of exploitation, both can be applied to a structured list of possible controls to assess the current state of security, and the directions that need to be investigated.

**All successful intrusions share the following characteristic phases [010]:**

❖ Reconnaissance
❖ Assessment and Strategy
❖ Exploitation / Invasion
❖ Maintaining Access

**Operations**

Attackers place different priorities on each stage. In essence, the more time spent on one step ensures better results in the following steps. Also, each phase is conducted in such a way as to ease the way for the next step, and lower the chance of getting caught.

**2.5.1 Reconnaissance, Assessment and Strategy**

Attacks don't just happen. They are preceded by a phase of information collection. Potential attackers scan and probe the target network for potential vulnerabilities to determine which type of attack to attempt [011].

Reconnaissance, or Recon, is the act of scoping out a target. This information gathering stage is the most important step an attacker takes, and all key information is considered. The Assessment and Strategy stage is the sorting of the gathered data to piece together an idea of what the hacker is attacking [010].

Recon can go undetected for considerable lengths of time and the Assessment and Strategy stage is often completely undetectable, as it is usually done without contact with the target.

26

These two stages are assessed together because Recon is the part of the act that involves interaction of some sort with the target, and the Assessment and Strategy stage is usually done remotely by reviewing the gathered data.

To launch successful attacks, attackers need information about the topology of the network, about accessible network services, about software versions, about valid user/password credentials, and about anything else that will help them succeed in their efforts.

Without such information, it is virtually impossible to successfully attack a network. Unlike attacks themselves, reconnaissance can only be performed in some very basic ways. These reconnaissance methods may change subtly over time, but they inevitably share some basic attributes. Typical recon techniques include [011]:

❖ **TCP/UDP port scan:** This method accounts for at least 70% of all recon activity. Port scan consists of sending a message to each port, one at a time. The kind of response received indicates whether the port is used and can therefore be probed for weakness. This is extremely valuable information, since it reveals any applications running on the host that are accessible from the network. The attacker can gain the information about "listening" or "open" ports. This is a list of programs on the system that will respond to network requests as there are well-known port numbers common to all hosts. There is no way to stop someone from port scanning a computer while a host is on the Internet because accessing an Internet server opens a port, which opens a door to that host.

❖ **NetBIOS probes:** NetBIOS probes interrogate an IP host for computer names, user names, shared resources (such as shared folders or printers), and so forth. Responses to such probes will disclose the fact that the probed IP host actually runs a NetBIOS layer, and will reveal the objects sought by the attacker. NetBIOS probe can provide valuable information about the host's status and help the attacker to find out weaknesses of the host.

❖ **SNMP probes:** These probes capitalize on the Simple Network Management Protocol (SNMP), which is used almost universally for communication between networked devices and management consoles. SNMP carries information about the nature, configuration, topology and health of those devices. As a result, attackers can gain a plethora of valuable information about all types of network resources like router table.

### 2.5.2 Exploitation and Invasion

Once an attacker has gathered enough information and has pieced together a reasonable amount of information about the network or system they are attacking, and have devised an initial plan of attack, it is then possible to begin the Exploitation and Invasion stage. At this point, the attacker uses the gathered knowledge and attempts to access the server through the channels that were found open [010]. In this phase, the intruder has gained access to desired system facilities. Penetration and exploitation create a spiral of increasing intruder authority and a widening circle of compromise. For example, penetration at the user level is typically a means to find root-level vulnerabilities. User-level authorization is then employed to exploit those vulnerabilities to achieve root-level privileges. Finally, compromise of the weakest host in a networked system allows that host to be used as a stepping-stone to compromise other more protected hosts. The success of this stage is mainly depends on the time spend on the recon stage and the experience of the attacker in well assigning the target host.

### 2.5.3 Maintaining Access

Once an attacker has penetrated the network (or if the attack is an inside job) steps are usually taken to make future accesses easier to conduct. This often includes installing a back-door program, but sometimes may be something as simple as setting up a home base under a seldom-used account name or identifying a misconfigured user account with suitable permissions to use to regain entry [010]. Attackers install tools and manipulate existing software on a system to maintain access to the machine on their own terms.

They install backdoors, apply "rootkits" (the process of substituting binary executables with nasty variations), and sometimes even manipulate the underlying kernel itself to hide their evil deeds. Attackers also cover their tracks by hiding files, sniffers, network usage, and running processes. Finally, attackers often alter system logs, all in an attempt to make the compromised system appear normal.

### 2.5.4 Operations

This is the most dangerous part of a penetration; the attacker has all the access required to carry out his/her plan. If it is a spy operation, data could be sent to a remote collection repository [012]. While this process does not give a concrete damage, it can damage the trust on the organization, and this will be reflected to the finance of that organization. Sometimes, this financial effect could be so harmful that it could lead to the bankruptcy of that organization. If the attack is a system-mapping reconnaissance mission, existing levels of access may be used to compromise more systems on the network [012]. This mapping process can be used to find out the weaknesses of the systems to gain access to them.

Then, those compromised systems, then, can be used to create a distributed denial of service (DDoS) attack. Or, that attack may be the first step for a spy operation and the compromised system could be used to gain access to more important systems on the network that could not be directly accessed.

Understanding the stages of attack process is central to effective defense. In fact, security administrators can take advantage of inherent flaws in the attack process to actually prevent attacks before they reach to its target. Just as attackers exploit vulnerabilities in the network to mount attacks, security administrators can exploit vulnerabilities in the attack process to protect themselves.

In each stage of an attack, there is the risk of exploitation. The types of exploits are [010]:

**1. Confidentiality–** implies that the information be agreed exclusively is same as the authorized person.

**2. Integrity–** consists of the need to maintain the stable information.

**3. Availability–** refers to the need to offer a service uninterruptedly, so that can be agreed in any moment and since any place, avoiding the possible thing that some type of incident stop it.

**4. Authenticity–** assures that the information is from the source that it claims to be from.

Security is defined through a "triad of concepts". The stage of the attack plus the type of exploit identifies the risk. As an example, in reconnaissance an attacker is primarily collecting data. There is no intention to alter data integrity or availability, although confidentiality is affected. Therefore at the reconnaissance stage of the attack, there is a risk of loss of confidentiality. At the other end of the scale stands, the operations stage where the attacker performs his or her intent. If he is spying, confidentiality is at risk. If he is malicious and intends on causing damage to the company, integrity and availability are at risk. This may also be the case, if the attacker intends only to spy, but mistakes made along the way have affected integrity and availability.

Strictly speaking, a control is a mechanism to reduce risk. This may entail blocking data flow to outside networks, ensuring data integrity, or maintaining its accessibility. Controls also provide functions to notify when an attempt has been made to circumvent allowable access, and an audit trail to accurately document differences. Most controls are focused on a limited number of threats or vulnerabilities, and singularly can be defeated. Because of this, a robust suite of controls is necessary to mitigate risk [010].

**There are five categories of controls:**

**1. Deterrence–** discourage individuals from intentionally violating information security policies or procedures

**2. Prevention–** avoid the occurrence of unwanted events

3. Detection– identify unwanted events after they have occurred

**4. Correction–** remedy the circumstances that allowed the unauthorized activity or return conditions to what they were before the violation

**5. Recovery–** restore lost computing resources or capabilities and help the organization recover monetary losses caused by a security violation

A gap in any one of the risk-control areas during any phase of an attack, as described above, is potential security vulnerability. Vulnerability is a security hole in computer operating systems, system software, or application software. Attackers exploit vulnerabilities to gain control of, damage, or bring down a device on the network. Threats to computing systems are circumstances that have the potential to cause loss or harm, such as human attacks, natural disasters, inadvertent human errors, and internal hardware and software flaws. "A control is a protective measure – an action, device, procedure, or technique – that reduces vulnerability" [013].

### 2.6 SPAM

The SPAM is a part of Hawaii's food legacy. Hawaii is the SPAM capital of the United States of America. SPAM was a luncheon meat made by George A. Hormel & Company in Austin, Minnesota. For the local residents of Hawaii, SPAM is SPAM and no other Luncheon meat can ever be passed of as SPAM. Mr. Kenneth Daugneau won a prize of $100.00 in a contest way back in year 1937, for suggesting a name SPAM(for spiced HAM). The SPAM became the king of canned meat in Hawaii. Whatever you are going to order in a Hawaiian restaurant, you will be having SPAM in that. (Corum) [014]

The Spam Track at the Text Retrieval Conference (TREC) defines email spam as-

"Unsolicited, unwanted email that was sent indiscriminately, directly, or indirectly, by a sender having no current relationship with the recipient."(Lynam) [015].

"The Spam is information crafted to be delivered to a large number of recipients, in spite of their wishes. A spam filter is an automated tool to recognize spam so as to prevent its delivery. The purposes of spam and spam filters are diametrically opposed: spam is effective if it evades filters, while a filter is effective if it recognizes spam. The circular nature of these definitions, along with their appeal to the intent of sender and recipient make them difficult to formalize." [016]

"Yet, current spam filters are remarkably effective, more effective than might be expected given the level of uncertainty and debate over a formal definition of spam, more effective than might be expected given the state-of-the-art information retrieval and machine learning methods for seemingly similar problems. But are they effective enough? Which are better? How might they be improved? Will their effectiveness be compromised by more cleverly crafted spam?" [016].

### 2.6.1   The Purpose of Spam

The motivation behind spam is to have information delivered to the recipient that contains a payload such as advertising for a (likely worthless, illegal, or non-existent) product, bait for a fraud scheme, promotion of a cause, or computer malware designed to hijack the recipient's computer. Because it is so cheap to send information, only a very small fraction of targeted recipients — perhaps one in ten thousand or fewer — need to receive and respond to the payload for spam to be profitable to its sender (Mangalindan) [017].

Now, spamming has become more sophisticated and specialized with better hidden payloads and more wicked purposes. Now spam sent in support of organized criminal activities, like hijacking computers, user's identity theft, trafficking illegal goods and services, etc. Computer viruses are crafted these days to hijack computers, to aid in identity theft and the propagation of more spam.

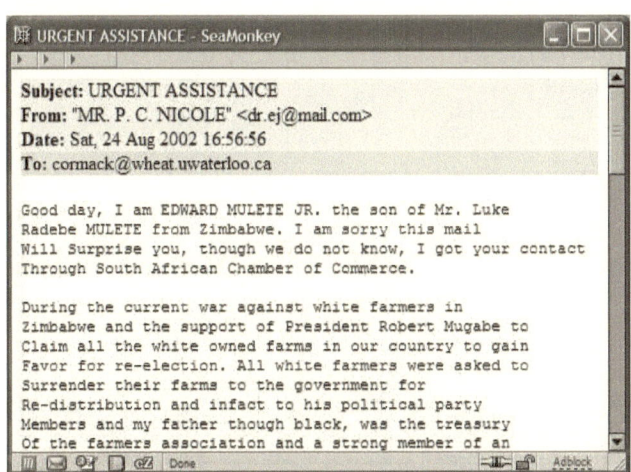

Figure 3 : Example of Identity Theft SPAM

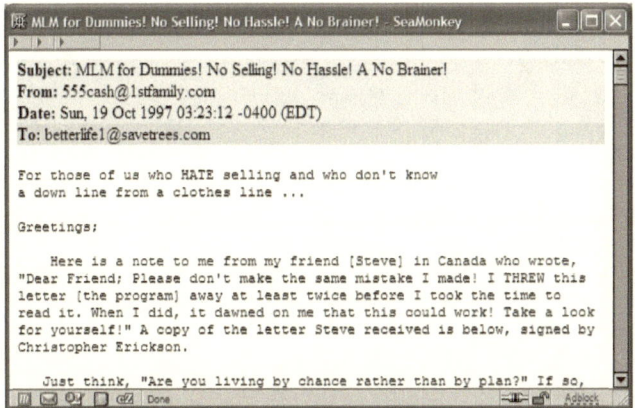

Figure 4 : Example of Chain Letters SPAM

Figure 5 : Example of SPAM spreading Virus

## 2.7 Characteristics of SPAM

Spam In any form should share some common characteristics:

### 2.7.1 Unwanted

Obviously the spam messages are unwanted as reported by the majority of recipients. Still some people takes spam positively, as observed that some spam campaigns work. Out of them some users later regrets for responding to Spam emails. The specific individuals may be looking for trafficking of illegal goods and services; still most of receivers reported them as unwanted. There are a large number of recipients who even failed to decide if they want the spam messages or don't want them, this is a class of novice users who are exploring the new trends and not well verse about the cyber crimes due to spammers.

### 2.7.2 Indiscriminate

There is no reason why Spam is transmitted between the sender and the receiver. It is more cost effective to send more spam than to be selective on target users. A spam message is automatically or semi-automatically made for its target is indiscriminate. For example, a spam email may include the name of recipient as a salutation of email so that receiver will feel that this email was tailored only for them. Such tailor made messages are sent just to disguise the indiscriminate targeting.

### 2.7.3 Disingenuous

As the spam is indiscriminate and unwanted, it must disguise such that spam emails should be delivered to masses and they should act upon the spam contents. There are unlimited possible methods to disguise the recipients and can't be enumerated. The most straightforward approach is to send spam emails with such subject and material so that it appears to be legitimate message.

You may receive a message that some of your colleague is travelling abroad and lost his money, so you may deposit some handsome money in an account so that he can come back. Such colleague should exist in your recent email list so that it will appear as legitimate to some of the recipients. Spam may disguise itself to appear as legitimate to spam filters by used misspelled words, noisy images containing embedded messages and using newly hijacked workstations to send messages are common spam characteristics which designed to disguise spam filters.

### 2.7.4 Bearing the Payload

The Spam message's payload may be hidden or visible still we can reduce the spam if we can identify the payload and what is the profit of spammer. These payloads may be in form of Website addresses, Name of products, contact informations, in plain text or images. Spam filters cannot read the text in form of images. Sometimes payload is just a message just to insure the validity of recipients email addresses or just to check the existence of spam filter, so that the spam detecting ability gets compromised.

## 2.8 SPAM Filtering

The Spam filtering is an automated technique to identity SPAM and HAM (Non-Spam). In general Spam filter is taking its decision about SPAM / HAM on the basis of message contents, on basis of characteristics of sender and receiver, having knowledge or experience if others have reported similar messages as Spam or not. As no one is perfect, so does the Spam filters, therefore we need to change the working of Spam Filters by adding some more constraints. We need to use different Spam Sets made available by some international spam research organizations such as :

- ❖ UCI Machine Learning Repository Spambase Data set (Mark Hopkins)
- ❖ The Enron-Spam Datasets (Enron)
- ❖ CSMINING Group Spam Email datasets (Group, p. CS MInining)
- ❖ SPAM Archive (Untroubled)

etc.

Internet Service Providers are widely using Automated and Semi-automated filtering solutions for corporate email solutions and premium individual customers. Completely automated solutions usually bounce or delete every suspected spam, where semi-automated solutions put aside possible and suspected spam for a human examination. The most common filtering solutions involve filtering email messages from already known spam senders based on Spam datasets according to the information stored in email headers or address sections. In addition to this, pattern matching modules can identify spam on the basis of information contained within the an email message body. It is practically tough to detect Spam on the basis of message text, as Spammers can easily dupe such pattern matchers. It is a serious blunder if any automated filter incorrectly identifies a single desired email as a spam. Also, there can be some legitimate messages that are sent simultaneously to thousands of recipients.

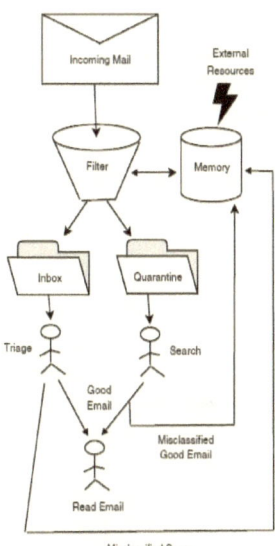

Figure 6 : Process of Spam Filtering

## 2.9 The State of Perimeter Security

In a physical structure, such as a building, strong materials for construction are used to provide the necessary security. By means of security, windows are located so that thieves cannot access them easily; barriers are placed around the building and access is controlled on each entry. Besides these, systems of caution, alarms and cameras are placed to monitor the inside, in addition to properly equipped personnel, continuously, patrolling the installation. Similar to physical security, information security managers have utilized multiple technologies to keep their networks safe. However, as an effect of the improvements in technology, networks are now connected to one or more outside networks – including, of course, the Internet. Hence, the corporations face with a wide range of threats. The fact that internal systems are actually quite vulnerable to all kinds of exploits makes these threats even worse. Plus, the widespread availability of reconnaissance tools has made it easier than ever for even novice attackers to bypass the enterprise security. So, security managers are under a lot of pressure to prevent any penetration to the network perimeter.

Luckily, similar to the physical security, there are numerous security tools to help security managers in setting up complex protection strategy plans for their computer systems. Mostly common ones are commented subsequently.

🔲

## 2.9.1 Firewalls

Firewalls are usually the first component of any perimeter defense. Firewalls provide a barrier of security among networks of different levels of confidence or security, utilizing network level access control politics. The major functional requirement of a firewall is to protect a private (internal) network from unauthorized external access.

Firewalls act like traffic cops and perform the critical task of filtering traffic crossing the network boundary. This filtering is done according to predefined security policies, which can be specified at the network layer and/or at the application layer. Firewalls utilize these static, manually configured, security policies to differentiate legitimate traffic from non-legitimate traffic.

**Typical reasons for using a firewall to protect a private network include the following [018]:**

- ❖ To prevent unauthorized external users from accessing computing resources on the internal network. This is necessary because it is extremely difficult and costly to attempt to secure all the hosts within a private network,
- ❖ To control internal user access to the external network to prevent the export of proprietary information,
- ❖ To avoid the negative public relations impact of a break in,

❖ To provide a dependable and reliable connection to the Internet, so that employees do not implement their own insecure private connections.

Firewalls must be installed at the choke points to control network traffic and implement network security policy of the organization for its external network connections, especially for the Internet. Because many Internet-based services are inherently insecure, a firewall must help an organization to disable some services and restrict others according to the organizational security policy [019]. Firewalls achieve this by examining the source and destination of all incoming and outgoing network traffic. All network traffic must pass through the firewall, which ensures that only permitted traffic are allowed through [020].

Set of rules specifies which packets can pass, which cannot. For example, a request addressed to an email server is allowed through; a request addressed to the corporate accounting system is denied. Usually, traffic destined for a Web server (port 80) or an email server (port 25) is granted access. Unless you specify otherwise, a firewall typically blocks all traffic addressed to other locations (i.e., servers, databases, or application servers) on the network, thus protecting those hosts against unauthorized external access.

There are various firewall products but they are grouped into three major types based on their mechanisms: packet filtering, Stateful inspection, and proxying.

### 2.9.2 Intrusion Detection System

A second layer in the perimeter defense is intrusion detection systems (IDSs). The audits of security existed before the intrusion detection. Audit is the process of generating, storing and revising events of a system chronologically. IDS is the evolved version of the traditional audits [021]. The term audit, in Latin "audire" (to hear), is defined as "to examine the economic management of a company in order to verify if it is adjusted to the established rules by law or custom" [022]. Intrusion detection is the process of monitoring and searching networks of computers and systems for security policy violations [023]. Intrusion Detection Systems (IDSs) are software or hardware

39

products that automate this monitoring and analysis process. An IDS inspects all inbound and outbound network activity, system logs and events, and identifies suspicious patterns or events that may indicate a network or system attack from someone attempting to break into or compromise a system [024].

Theoretically, IDSs work like a burglar alarm, alerting security managers that an attack may be taking place so that they can respond accordingly. IDSs trigger these alerts by detecting anomalous traffic patterns or "signatures" that are characteristic of an attack. As in the physical world, our logical burglar alarm provides valuable notification that someone has managed to breach perimeter security measures, and should allow security managers to determine exactly what happened during the attack, and hopefully provide indications of how the security weakness might be addressed.

IDSs have gained acceptance as a necessary addition to every organization's security infrastructure. Since they are first put on the security market, those organizations have several compelling reasons to acquire and use IDSs.

**Some of them are listed below [025]:**

- ❖ To prevent problematic behaviours by increasing the perceived risk of discovery and punishment for those who would attack or otherwise abuse the system,
- ❖ To detect attacks and other security violations that are not prevented by other security measures,
- ❖ To detect and deal with the preambles to attacks (commonly experienced as network probes and other reconnaissance activities),
- ❖ To document the existing threat to an organization,
- ❖ To act as quality control tool for security design and administration, especially for large and complex enterprises,
- ❖ To provide useful information about intrusions that take place, allowing detailed analysis, recovery, and correction of causative factors.

## 2.10 Honeypots

A third security technology being used by many organizations is honeypots. A honeypot is a system or dataset for which there is no legitimate reason for someone to interact with it and therefore all use can be considered unauthorized [026]. Honeypots are installed behind a firewall, although is also possible to situate them in front of them.

"Honey Pot Systems [026] are decoy servers or systems setup to gather information regarding an attacker or intruder into your system. It is important to remember that Honey Pots do not replace other traditional Internet security systems; they are an additional level or system".

"Honey Pots can be setup inside, outside or in the DMZ of a firewall design or even in all of the locations although they are most often deployed inside of a firewall for control purposes. In a sense, they are variants of standard Intruder Detection Systems (IDS) but with more of a focus on information gathering and deception [026]."

**Honeypots are designed to [027]:**

divert an attacker from accessing critical systems, collect information about the attacker's activity, and encourage the attacker to stay on the system long enough for security managers to respond."[028]

"Honeypots are highly flexible security tools with different applications for security. Unlike firewalls or IDSs, honeypots do not solve a specific problem. Instead, they have multiple uses, such as prevention, detection, or information gathering. There are various implementations but they all share the same concept: a security resource that should not have any production or authorized activity. Theoretically, a honeypot should see no traffic because it has no legitimate activity. This means any interaction with a honeypot is most likely unauthorized or malicious activity [029]. Any connection attempts to a honeypot are most likely a probe, attack, or compromise. This is what a honeypot is, it is a security resource whose value lies in being probed, attacked, or compromised. Honeypots in a network should not affect critical network services and applications. Such characteristics clearly distinguish honeypots than other security solutions" [029].

"An example of a Honey Pot systems installed in a traditional Internet security design:

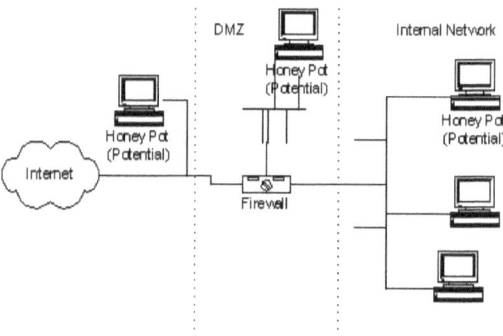

Figure 7: A Honeypot (www.sans.org) [008]

"Honeypots only capture bad activity; any interaction with a honeypot is most likely unauthorized or malicious activity. Thus, honeypots collect small data sets having high value, as the data set contains only the attacks. This means it's much easier (and cheaper) to analyze the data a honeypot collects and derives value from it" [029].

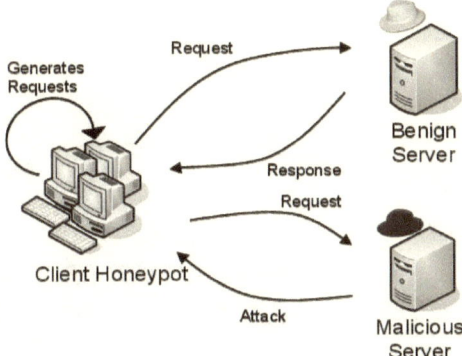

Figure 8 : Client Honeypot (Project)[030]

**Implementing a honeypot is very easy. The following steps specify an example implementation of a honeypot [030]:**

"Install the operating system without patches installed and using typical defaults and options,"[030]

"Make sure that there is no data on the system that cannot safely be destroyed,"[030]

"Add the application that is designed to record the activities of the invader."[030]

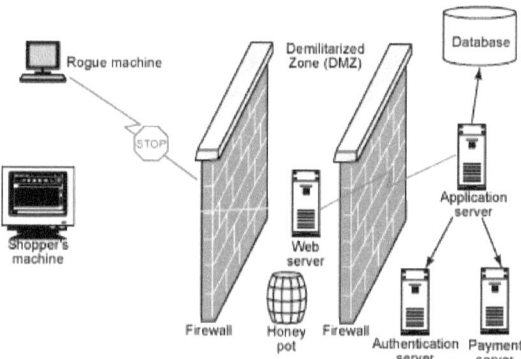

Figure 9: Firewalls and Honeypots [031]

A system which is simulating one or more than one network services on a host can be an example of Honeypot. An attacker can assume that spam bot can break into vulnerable services which can be used to break into it. "Such Honeypot can be used to log access attempts to those ports including the attacker's keystrokes" [026]. This could give security managers advanced warning of a more concerted attack. That is what we use honeypots.

Honeypots can be divided into two types: production and research. Production honeypots are easy to use, capture only limited information, and are used primarily by companies or corporations, help preventing, detecting, or responding to an attack Research honeypots are complex to deploy and maintain, capture extensive information, and are used primarily by research, military, or government organizations [026]. They are used to collect information. That information can be used in early warning and prediction, law enforcement or understanding trends in attacker activity.

**Some of the advantages and disadvantages associates to them are described subsequently:**

**Advantages:**

"Honeypots lure attackers by presenting a more visible and apparently vulnerable resource than the enterprise network itself. Thus, they distract attackers from more valuable hosts on the network" [032],

Honeypots are used in detecting attacks, as they can be monitored for a proof of anomalous activities by security managers.

"Honeypots are useful for forensics, since they can be specifically designed to retain data pertaining to an attack" [032].

Honeypots allow in-depth examination of attacks during and after exploitation of the targets,

"Unlike most security technologies (such as IDS systems) honeypots work fine in encrypted or IPv6 environments" [029],

Honeypots can be used provide an early warning about new attacks and their exploitation trends.

"Besides, it should not be forgotten that attackers don't have to focus on a limited number of targets with today's automated tools. They can attack the honeypot and the enterprise network – and anything else in sight. In fact, if they are incorrectly configured, honeypots can actually make the enterprise more vulnerable to attack by virtue of being linked logically to it [032]". Therefore, a high level of expertise is needed for administrators and security managers in order to use these systems.

Application communications may be tracked to identify abnormal application behaviour and a network security administrator may be notified that a particular application may be notified that a particular application may be making the network vulnerable to intrusion. Immediate response to abnormal application behaviour or detection of an intrusion signature is made possible, while non-targeted applications on a targeted computing system may continue their network activity. [114]

# CHAPTER – 03

# DISTRIBUTED DENIAL OF SERVICE ATTACKS

## 3.1 Classification of DDoS Attacks

The DDoS field is evolving quickly, and it is becoming increasingly hard to grasp a global view of the problem. This study strives to introduce some structure to the DDoS field by proposing a classification of DDoS attacks and DDoS defense systems. [033]

This study has not been done to propose or advocate any specific DDoS defense mechanism. Some sections might point out vulnerabilities of certain defense systems, but our purpose is not to criticize but to draw attention to these problems.

The main purpose of this study [033] is to provide a clear and thorough coverage of the area of DDoS attacks. In principle, this study attempts to aid the DDoS research on the issues related to the field of attack mechanisms. The study is based on a comprehensive literature review, which spans an area of source codes and analyses of DDoS attack tools.

**The prime objectives of this research can be summarized to the following:**

Analyse the details of DDoS attack mechanisms and the principles DDoS attacks rely,

Present the novel classification of DDoS attack mechanisms,

Discuss a few of the possible evolutions of the DDoS attack mechanisms.

## 3.2 The DDoS Attack Problem

The definition provided by [034] is the definition for denial-of-service attack used in this research:

"A denial-of-service attack is characterized by an exclusive function of the attack and an explicit attempt by one or more attackers to prevent one or more legitimate users of a service from using that service."

46

A denial-of-service attack is characterized by an explicit attempt by attackers to prevent legitimate users of a service from using that service [034]. A DDoS attack deploys multiple machines to attain this goal. The service is denied by sending a stream of packets to a victim that either consumes some key resource, thus rendering it unavailable to legitimate clients, or provides the attacker with unlimited access to the victim machine so he can inflict arbitrary damage. In Fig. 7 "Ping of Death" type DDoS attack in shown.

### 3.3 The DDoS Attack Strategy

In order to perform a distributed denial-of-service attack, the attacker needs to recruit the multiple agent (slave) machines. This process is usually performed automatically through scanning of remote machines, looking for security holes that would enable subversion. Vulnerable machines are then exploited by using the discovered vulnerability to gain access to the machine and they are infected with the attack code. The exploit/infection phase is also automated and the infected machines can be used for further recruitment of new agents.

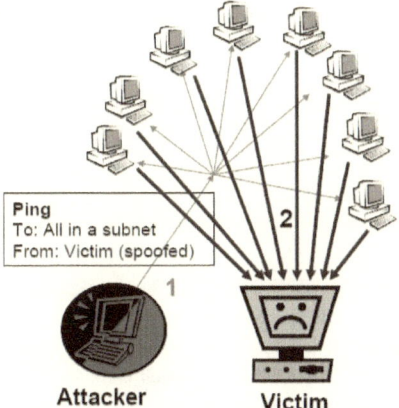

Figure 10: A Type of DDoS Attack e.g. "Ping of Death

47

Agent machines perform the attack against the victim. Attackers usually hide the identity of the agent machines during the attack through spoofing of the source address field in packets. The agent machines can thus be reused for future attacks.

### 3.4 Classification of DDoS Attacks

To classify the DDoS Attacks, the information on which the classification was built was gathered from live and publicly available DDoS attack tools. The source code of the tools used as references are: [035], [036], [037], [038], [039], [040], [041], [042], [043], [044], [045], [046], [047] and [048]. Analysis of DDoS attack tools used as references are Trinity [049], Shaft [050], Power bot [051] and GT bot [052].

**There are three general categories of attacks:**

❖ Against users
❖ Against hosts
❖ fork() bomb

Intentionally generate errors to fill logs, consuming disk space, crashing

❖ The power switch!!
❖ Against networks
❖ UDP bombing
❖ TCP SYN flooding
❖ Ping of death
❖ Smurf attack

### 3.4.1 Classification by Degree of Automation

During the attack preparation, the attacker needs to locate prospective agent machines and infect them with the attack code. Based on the degree of automation of the attack, we differentiate between following:

### Manual Attacks

The attacker scanned remote machines for vulnerabilities, broke into them and installed the attack code, and then commanded the onset of the attack. The early DDoS attacks belong to this category. There comes the need of automation in DDoS attacks.

### Semi-Automatic Attacks

The DDoS network consists of handler (master) and agent (slave, daemon) machines. The attacker deploys automated scripts for scanning and compromise of those machines and installation of the attack code. He then uses handler machines to specify the attack type and the victim's address and to command the onset of the attack to agents, who send packets to the victim.

### Automatic Attacks

Automatic DDoS attacks additionally automate the attack phase, thus avoiding the need for communication between attacker and agent machines. The time of the onset of the attack, attack type, duration and victim's address is pre-programmed in the attack code. It is obvious that such deployment mechanisms offer minimal exposure to the attacker, since he is only involved in issuing a single command – the start of the attack script. The hardcoded attack specification suggests a single-purpose use of the DDoS network. However, the propagation mechanisms usually leave the backdoor to the compromised machine open, enabling easy future access and modification of the attack code.

Both semi-automatic and automatic attacks recruit the agent machines by deploying automatic scanning and propagation techniques.

### 3.4.2 Classification by Scanning Strategy

**Attacks with Random Scanning**

During random scanning each compromised host probes random addresses in the IP address space, using a different seed. This potentially creates a high traffic volume since many machines probe the same addresses. The Code Red 'CRv2' is an example of Random Scanning. [053]

**Attacks with Hit-list Scanning**

A machine performing hit-list scanning probes all addresses from an externally supplied list. When it detects the vulnerable machine, it sends one half of the initial hit-list to the recipient and keeps the other half.

**Attacks with Topological Scanning**

Topological scanning uses the information on the compromised host to select new targets. All Email worms use topological scanning, exploiting the information from address books for their spread.

**Attacks with Permutation Scanning**

During permutation scanning, all compromised machines share a common pseudo-random permutation of the IP address space; each IP address is mapped to an index in this permutation. A machine begins scanning by using the index computed from its IP address as a starting point. Whenever it sees an already infected machine, it chooses a new random start point. This has the effect of providing a semi-coordinated, comprehensive scan while maintaining the benefits of random probing.

**Attacks with Local Subnet Scanning**

Local subnet scanning can be added to any of the previously described techniques to preferentially scan for targets that reside on the same subnet as the compromised host. Using this technique, a single copy of the scanning program can compromise many vulnerable machines behind a firewall. Code

50

Red II [054] and Nimda Worm [055] used local subnet scanning. Based on the attack code propagation mechanism, we differentiate between attacks that deploy central source propagation, back-chaining propagation and autonomous propagation [056].

### 3.4.3    Classification by Propagation Mechanism

**Attacks with Central Source Propagation**

During central source propagation, the attack code resides on a central server or set of servers. After compromise of the agent machine, the code is downloaded from the central source through a file transfer mechanism. The 1i0n [057] worm operated in this manner.

Attacks with Back-chaining Propagation

During back-chaining propagation, the attack code is downloaded from the machine that was used to exploit the system. The infected machine then becomes the source for the next propagation step.   Back-chaining propagation is more survivable than central-source propagation since it avoids a single point of failure. The Ramen worm [058] and Morris Worm [059] used backchaining propagation.

**Attacks with Autonomous Propagation**

Autonomous propagation avoids the file retrieval step by injecting attack instructions directly into the target host  during  the  exploitation phase. Code Red [060], Warhol Worm [061] and  numerous E-mail worms use autonomous propagation.

### 3.4.4  Classification by Communication Mechanism

**Attacks with direct communication**

During attacks with direct communication, the agent and handler machines need to know each other's identity in order to communicate. This is achieved by hard-coding the IP address of the handler machines in the attack code that is later installed on the agent. Each agent then reports its readiness to the handlers, who store its IP address in a file for later communication. The obvious drawback of this approach is that discovery of one compromised machine can expose the whole DDoS network. Also, since agents and handlers listen to network connections, they are identifiable by network scanners. A Direct DDoS Attack is shown in Fig. 8

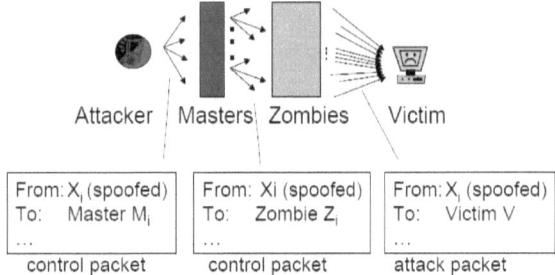

Figure 11: A Direct DDoS Attack

**Attacks with indirect communication**

Attacks with indirect communication deploy a level of indirection to increase the survivability of a DDoS network. Recent attacks provide the example of using IRC channels [062] for agent/handler communication. The use of IRC services replaces the function of a handler, since the IRC channel offers sufficient anonymity to the attacker. Since DDoS agents establish outbound connections to a standard service port used by a legitimate network service, agent communications to the control point may not be easily differentiated from legitimate network traffic. An attacker controls the agents using IRC communications channels. A Reflector DDoS Attack is shown in Fig. 9

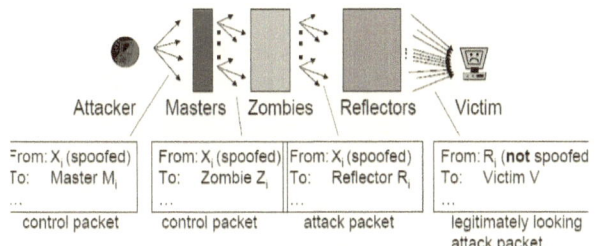

Figure 12 : A Reflector DDoS Attack

### 3.4.5  Classification by Exploited Vulnerability

**Protocol Attacks**

Protocol attacks exploit a specific feature or implementation bug of some protocol installed at the victim in order to consume excess amounts of its resources. Examples include the TCP SYN attack, the CGI request attack and the authentication server attack.

In the TCP SYN attack, the exploited feature is the allocation of substantial space in a connection queue immediately upon receipt of a TCP SYN request. The attacker initiates multiple connections that are never completed, thus filling up the connection queue indefinitely.

In the CGI request attack, the attacker consumes the CPU time of the victim by issuing multiple CGI requests.

In the authentication server attack, the attacker exploits the fact that the signature verification process consumes significantly more resources than bogus signature generation. He sends numerous bogus authentication requests to the server, tying up its resources.

**Brute-force Attacks**

Brute-force attacks are performed by initiating a vast amount of seemingly legitimate transactions. Since an upstream network can usually deliver higher traffic volume than the victim network can handle, this exhausts the victim's resources.

**Filterable Attacks**

Filterable attacks use bogus packets or packets for non-critical services of the victim's operation, and thus can be filtered by a firewall. Examples of such attacks are a UDP flood attack or an ICMP request flood attack on a Web server.

**Non-filterable Attacks**

Non-filterable attacks use packets that request legitimate services from the victim. Thus, filtering all packets that match the attack signature would lead to an immediate denial of the specified service to both attackers and the legitimate clients. Examples are a HTTP request flood targeting a Web server or a DNS request flood targeting a name server.

The line between protocol and brute force attacks is thin. Protocol attacks also overwhelm a victim's resources with excess traffic, and badly designed protocol features at remote hosts are frequently used to perform "reflector" brute-force attacks, such as the DNS request attack [063]or the Smurf attack [064]. The difference is that a victim can mitigate the effect of protocol attacks by modifying the deployed protocols at its site, while it is helpless against brute-force attacks due to their misuse of legitimate services (non-filterable attacks) or due to its own limited resources (a victim can do nothing about an attack that swamps its network bandwidth).

Countering protocol attacks by modifying the deployed protocol pushes the corresponding attack mechanism into the brute-force category. For example, if the victim deploys TCP SYN cookies [065] to combat TCP SYN attacks, it will still be vulnerable to TCP SYN attacks that generate more requests than its network can accommodate.

It is interesting to note that the variability of attack packet contents is determined by the exploited vulnerability. Packets comprising protocol and non-filterable brute force attacks must specify some valid header fields and possibly some valid contents. For example TCP SYN attack packets cannot vary the protocol or flag field, and HTTP flood packets must belong to an established TCP connection and therefore cannot spoof source addresses, unless they hijack connections from legitimate clients.

### 3.5 Overview of DDoS Tools

Attackers follow trends in the network security field and adjust their attacks to defeat current defense mechanisms. We now provide a quick overview of the several well-known DDoS attack tools in order to illustrate the variety of mechanisms deployed.

Trinoo [066] is a simple tool used to launch coordinated UDP flood attacks against one or many IP addresses. The attack uses constant-size UDP packets to target random ports on the victim machine. The handler uses UDP or TCP to communicate with the agents. This channel can be encrypted and password protected as well. Trinoo does not spoof source addresses although it can easily be extended to include this capability.

Tribe Flood Network (TFN) [067] can generate UDP and ICMP echo request floods, TCP SYN floods and ICMP directed broadcast (e.g., Smurf). It can spoof source IP addresses and also randomize the target ports. Communication between handlers and agents occurs exclusively through ICMP_ECHO_REPLY packets.

Stacheldraht [068] combines features of Trinoo (handler/agent architecture) with those of the original TFN (ICMP/TCP/UDP flood and Smurf style attacks). It adds encryption to the communication channels between the attacker and Stacheldraht handlers. Communication is performed through TCP and ICMP packets. It allows automated update of the agents using rcp and a stolen account at some site as a cache. New program versions will have more features and different signatures to avoid detection.

TFN2K [069] is the variant of TFN that includes features designed specifically to make TFN2K traffic difficult to recognize and filter. Targets are attacked via UDP, TCP SYN, ICMP_ECHO flood or Smurf attack, and the attack type can be varied during the attack. Commands are sent from the handler to the agent via TCP, UDP, ICMP, or all three at random. The command packets may be interspersed with any number of decoy packets sent to random IP addresses to avoid detection. TFN2K can forge packets that appear to come from neighbouring machines. All communication between handlers and agents is encrypted and base-64 encoded.

The mstream [070] tool uses spoofed TCP packets with the ACK flag set to attack the target. Communication is not encrypted and is performed through TCP and UDP packets. Access to the handler is password protected. This program has a feature not found in other DDoS tools. It informs all connected users of access, successful or not, to the handler(s) by competing parties.

Shaft [071] uses TCP, ICMP or UDP flood to perform the attack, and it can deploy all three styles simultaneously. UDP is used for communication between handlers and agents, and messages are not encrypted. Shaft randomizes the source IP address and the source port in packets. The size of packets remains fixed during the attack. A new feature is the ability to switch the handler's IP address and port during the attack.

The Code Red [072] worm is self-propagating malicious code that exploits a known vulnerability in Microsoft IIS servers for propagation. It achieves a synchronized attack by pre-programming the onset and abort time of the attack, attack method and target addresses (i.e., no handler/agent architecture is involved).

## 3.6 Classification of DDoS Defence Mechanisms

The seriousness of the DDoS problem and the increased frequency of DDoS attacks have led to the advent of numerous DDoS defense mechanisms. Some of these mechanisms address a specific kind of DDoS attack such as attacks on Web servers or authentication servers. Other approaches attempt to solve the entire generic DDoS problem. Most of the proposed approaches require certain features to achieve their peak performance, and will perform quite differently if deployed in an environment where these requirements are not met.

We need to understand not only each existing DDoS defense approach, but also how those approaches might be combined together to effectively and completely solve the problem. The proposed classification may help us reach this goal.

### 3.6.1. Classifications by Activity Level

**Preventive Mechanisms**

The goal of preventive mechanisms is either to eliminate the possibility of DDoS attacks altogether or to enable potential victims to endure the attack without denying services to legitimate clients. According to these goals we further divide preventive mechanisms into attack prevention and denial-of-service prevention mechanisms.

**Attack Prevention Mechanisms**

Attack prevention mechanisms modify the system configuration to eliminate the possibility of a DDoS attack.

**System Security Mechanisms**

Increase the overall security of the system, guarding against illegitimate accesses to the machine, removing application bugs and updating protocol installations to prevent intrusions and misuse of the system. DDoS attacks owe their power to large numbers of subverted machines that cooperatively generate the attack streams. If these machines were secured, the attackers would lose their army and the DDoS threat would then disappear.

**Protocol Security Mechanisms**

Protocol security mechanisms address the problem of bad protocol design. Many protocols contain operations that are cheap for the client but expensive for the server. Such protocols can be misused to exhaust the resources of a server by initiating large numbers of simultaneous transactions. Classic misuse examples are the TCP SYN attack, the authentication server attack, and the fragmented packet attack, in which the attacker bombards the victim with malformed packet fragments forcing it to waste its resources on reassembling attempts.

## Reactive Mechanisms

Reactive mechanisms strive to alleviate the impact of an attack on the victim. In order to attain this goal they need to detect the attack and respond to it. The goal of attack detection is to detect every attempted DDoS attack as early as possible and to have a low degree of false positives.

## Mechanisms with Pattern Attack Detection

Mechanisms that deploy pattern detection store the signatures of known attacks in a database. Each communication is monitored and compared with database entries to discover occurrences of DDoS attacks. Occasionally, the database is updated with new attack signatures. The obvious drawback of this detection mechanism is that it can only detect known attacks, and it is usually helpless against new attacks or even slight variations of old attacks that cannot be matched to the stored signature. On the other hand, known attacks are easily and reliably detected, and no false positives are encountered.

## Mechanisms with Anomaly Attack Detection

Mechanisms that deploy anomaly detection have a model of normal system behaviour, such as a model of normal traffic dynamics or expected system performance. The current state of the system is periodically compared with the models to detect anomalies.

## Mechanisms with Hybrid Attack Detection

Mechanisms that deploy hybrid detection combine the pattern-based and anomaly-based detection, using data about attacks discovered through an anomaly detection mechanism to devise new attack signatures and update the database.

### Mechanisms with Third-Party Attack Detection

Mechanisms that deploy third-party detection do not handle the detection process themselves, but rely on an external message that signals the occurrence of the attack and provides attack characterization.

### Agent Identification Mechanisms

Agent identification mechanisms provide the victim with information about the identity of the machines that are performing the attack. This information can then be combined with other response approaches to alleviate the impact of the attack.

### Filtering Mechanisms

Filtering mechanisms use the characterization provided by a detection mechanism to filter out the attack stream completely.

### Autonomous Mechanisms

Autonomous mechanisms perform independent attack detection and response. They are usually deployed at a single point in the Internet and act locally. Firewalls and intrusion detection systems provide an easy example of autonomous mechanisms.

### 3.6.2 Classification by Deployment Location

### Victim-Network Mechanisms

DDoS defence mechanisms deployed at the victim network protect this network from DDoS attacks and respond to detected attacks by alleviating the impact on the victim. Historically, most defence systems were located at the victim since it suffered the greatest impact of the attack and was therefore the most motivated to sacrifice some resources for increased security.

### Intermediate-Network Mechanisms

DDoS defense mechanisms deployed at the intermediate network provide infrastructural service to a large number of Internet hosts. Victims of DDoS attacks can contact the infrastructure and request the service, possibly providing adequate compensation.

### Source-Network Mechanisms

The goal of DDoS defense mechanisms deployed at the source network is to prevent customers using this network from generating DDoS attacks. Such mechanisms are necessary and desirable, but motivation for their deployment is low since it is unclear who would pay the expenses associated with this service.

### 3.7 Conclusion of Classification

Distributed denial of service attacks is a complex and serious problem and consequently, numerous approaches have been proposed to counter them. The multitude of current attack and defense mechanisms obscures the global view of the DDoS problem. It is important to recognize and understand trends in attack technology in order to effectively and appropriately evolve defense and response strategies.

The classifications described here are intended to think about the threats we face and the measures we can use to counter those threats. We do not claim that these classifications are complete and all-encompassing. Many more attack possibilities exist and must be addressed before we can completely handle the DDoS threat, and some of them are likely to be outside the current boundaries of the classification presented here. Thus, these taxonomies are likely to require expansion and refinement as new threats and defense mechanisms are discovered. The DDoS attack and DDoS defense classifications outlined in this research are useful to the extent that they clarify our thinking and guide us to more effective solutions to the problem of DDoS. The ultimate value of the work described here will thus be in the degree of discussion and future research that it provokes.

# CHAPTER – 04
# SPAM ATTACKS

## 4.1 Defining the Spam

The Spam is generally an unwanted, annoying commercial email. It generally consists of bogus offers and information's intended to spend your time and money. So just like uninvited telemarketing calls about different promotional offers try to limit the amount of spam mails you are getting.

"Many researchers have applied statistical analysis techniques to email for classification purposes, such as identifying spam messages. Such approaches can be highly effective, however many examine incoming email exclusively — which does not provide detailed information about an individual user's behavior. Only by analysing outgoing messages can a user's behavior be ascertained".[073]

Because of the Internet's intensive use and need of the time, an email has become as one of the fastest and an economical mode of communication. Which enables internet users to easily transfer information from anywhere in the world with in a fraction of second. As the number of email users is increasing exponentially there is also a dramatic increase of spam emails witnessed during the past few years. E-mail spam, which is also known as unsolicited bulk e-mail (UBE) or Junk Email, can be termed as a subset of spam which is devised to deliver almost identical messages to number of recipients by e-mail. Spam definition says that spam e-mail are sent in bulk and they are unsolicited. E-mail spam is steadily growning since early 1990s. More than 80% of Email Spams are sent from the Botnets or networks of virus-infected computer machines.

Spammers usually collect Email addresses from online chat rooms, yellow pages and other websites, published or unpublished customer lists, online newsgroups, and some viruses or worms which harvest users address books and they sold these addresses to other spammers for money. As recipient or end user mostly borne the cost of the spam, most of individuals and business organizations send emails in bulk in the form of spam. "The voluminous of spam emails a strain the Information Technology based organizations and creates billions of dollars lose in terms of productivity. In recent years, spam emails lands up into a serious security threat, and act as a prime medium for phishing of sensitive information". (M. Chandrasekaran, June, 2006). These days email classification becomes a growing research area to automatically classify legitimate emails from spam emails.

Spam email also fascinate problem for individuals and organizations because it is prone to misuse. Automatic email spam classification [076] contains more challenges because of unstructured information, more number of features and large number of documents. As the usage increases all of these features may adversely affect performance in terms of quality and speed. Many recent algorithms use only relevant features for classification. Even though more number of classification techniques has been developed for spam classification, still 100% accuracy of predicting the spam email is questionable. So Identification of best spam algorithm itself became a tedious task because of features and drawbacks of every algorithm against each other.

### 4.2 Growth of Spam Statistics

"Over the past few years, the volume of e-mail spam has grown significantly to the point it is no longer just a nuisance. Some reports suggest that as much as 90–95% of all e-mail sent or received today is spam". [074, 075]. "Today, botnets are widely used as a scalable and elusive approach to disseminating spam messages. Spammers purchase access to a fraction of bots controlled by the botnet to send out spam messages from the infected hosts.

Spammers send these instructions from the command and control (C&C) server via encrypted channels to the bots. Recently, spamming botnets have made the transition from proxy-based spamming to template-based spamming. These new sophisticated user interfaces play a key role in the efficiency of dissemination mechanisms in spamming infrastructures."[077] "These improvements have lead to an exponential increase in spamming capabilities. For example, "Srizbi" is claimed to be capable of sending 60 billion spam messages per day, which is more than half of the total 100 billion spam messages sent per day on average" [078]. "Another large-scale spamming botnet, "Conficker", consists of more than 10 million infected hosts all over the world and could be capable of sending out 400 billion spam messages per day" [079].

### 4.3 Common Practices to reduce the Spam :

### 4.3.1 Using Email-Filters:

Most of Email accounts are coming with spam filters to check potential spam or to transfer spam mails to a spam/bulk folder. You may select your Email service provider on this parameter if they are providing some spam filter or not. Some email service providers are giving another chance to such Spam mails by providing an option to categorize them as 'Not Spam' by the user.

### 4.3.2 By limiting your Surfing exposure:

One good idea is to use two different email addresses, oneyou're your personal messages and another for e-shopping, receive newsletters, access chat rooms, to get discount coupons etc. You may transfer important email messages to your main account from this secondary email address. Once your secondary address starts receiving spam, you may shut it down without affecting your main email address.

You should also avoid displaying your email address on publically accessible sections of any websites, i.e.don't mention your main email account on different blog posts, in public chat rooms, on popular social networking sites, or in online available membership directories. Spammers use the web to collect or harvest email addresses from these locations.

### 4.3.3 Check Privacy Policy sections on Websites:

You should read the privacy policy on websites before submitting your email address. If the company is selling or sharing your email address with others websites or displaying on social sites, you should not submit your email address to such websites which cannot protect your identity. If there is an already selected check-boxes on a website to sign up for email updates from this other partner companies.

### 4.3.4 Choose a unique email address:

Many spam clients makes different name combinations in order to find out a valid email address. Therefore, a common name such as manish may get more spam than a mani9477 type unique name which is sometimes harder to remember than previous one.

### 4.4 Practices to reduce Spam for others

It's a favourite pastime for Hackers and spammers to troll the internet. They keep looking for computers or machines that are not protected by any up-to-date security software or firewall. Whenever they find any unprotected computers, they try to install some hidden software – known as Malware, which allows the Spammers/Hackers to control these computers from remote locations for their malicious works. Such corrupted machines are known as 'Bots'.

These Spammers/Hackers make botnet's by making a network of bots, " The Botnet is a network used by spammers or hackers to send millions of junk emails at once. Millions of computers at your home or office place are part of such Botnets. Mostly these botnet activities are hidden from the owner of that machine. This is a type of Distributed Denial of Service attacks, as such bots are using your machine resources, Contact Lists, Hard Disk, RAM, Internet Bandwidth etc. Most of the spam is sent this way only."

### 4.4.1 Protect your computer to not let used by Spammers

By using following suggestions you can help to reduce the chances so that your computer should not become a part of botnet:

Use effective computer security practices and also disconnect your internet connection when you're not using or going away from your work station. Hackers cannot control your computer when it is disconnected from the internet.

Take due precautions while opening any email attachments or downloading files. If you are not sure about any attachment, don't open it.

Whenever you send an email with an attachment, always mention about the files it's including.

"There is no Free Lunch in this World !" don't expect free softwares on any website, there is almost no website which is launched to help you, there hidden agenda can be dangerous for your system resources. These free softwares may contain Malware's.

### 4.4.2 Detect and Remove Malware from your workstation

Though it can be difficult to find that if a spammer has installed Malware on your workstation, but still there are some symptoms :

Your Workstation is working slow or operating sluggishly.

Your friends are receiving weird email messages that you have never sent.

There are few emails in your sent folder which you have never sent.

Your Internet bandwidth is used even when you are not running any bandwidth consuming applications.

There is some unknown application running in your Task Manager status through your current user account which you have not started.

If your system is affected with any Malware first of all disconnect your system from Internet and then take security measures to remove them. Most of Anti-virus companies are exists online because they are themselves making viruses and displaying their advertisements in different websites claiming that they can remove Malware and Viruses from your machine free of cost.

### 4.4.3 Spam Reporting

If you are still receiving Spam Emails, you may inform your Email Service provider whenever you see a junk mail. Most of Email service providers are showing a button on every Email like, 'Report Spam'.

The Google's Penguin 2.0 update is aimed to reduce web spam and get quality sites to appear at the top of search results. However, there is always going to be a way to tilt the odds of ranking highly in your favour, which is what you're going to learn when you opt in to our post Penguin 2.0 SEO strategy email list. The original Penguin updated targeted on-site over-optimization. This means that if you have an unnatural amount of keywords that you were clearly trying to rank for, that you got penalized. For example if you were trying to rank for "Black shoes for men" and this exact keyphrase "Black shoes for men" appeared in your title tags, meta descriptions, H1, H2, H3 tags, in your footer and in every second sentence of your content, you would very likely have been slapped all the way down the rankings to a position where nobody will ever find you.[080]

"DISCOVER EXACTLY HOW OUR **RANKINGS INCREASED** *AFTER* PENGUIN 2.0 WITH **ACTUAL CASE STUDIES**"

Figure 13 Google Penguin 2.0

The core of SEO is highly unlikely to change. Google still uses an algorithm (code with rules to follow) to determine which sites to rank. That means there is a checklist of good and bad things that the Google bots and spiders look for, and if your site meets these good things on the checklist, you will be rewarded with high rankings. [080].

This is a great initiative taken by the Google by launching Penguin 2.0 update, who have started SEO concept, who is the leader in Online Marketing tools, who is responsible for creating Spams, who has given Google Adwords to give your Website top listings in Google Searches, who has given Google

Adsense so that you can earn by displaying your advertisements on other websites. Google is the biggest problem maker and now providing the remedy for problems created by it self. We can report Spam links and Websites through Google Penguin so that we can get genuine Websites on the top of searches.

Figure 14 Google WebSpam Report Plugin [081]

### 4.5 Top Ten SPAM Characteristics

Even though some spam messages are hard to distinguish from legitimate emails, most spam mails include 'tell-tale' signs that can be used to filter them out. Below mentioned are top 10 spam characteristics and how they can be used to detect spam. Some of these characteristics can also be present in legitimate mails. Therefore it is important to use a weighting system that provides an individual score for each spam characteristic. If a message includes several spam characteristics and reaches a 'spam threshold', the email can safely be considered as spam.

Here each spam characteristic is placed according to the frequency in which it is found in today's spam mails, where #1 is the spam characteristic that Red Earth Software found to be most common. (Patrol) (Patrol) [081]

**#10. Illegal HTML exists:** Some spam messages include a code for identification in the text of the message. The text is entered outside the HTML tags so as to hide the code from the recipient. There is no legitimate reason to add text outside HTML tags, so the mere presence of illegal HTML can be treated as suspicious.

**#9. Message body contains small font size:** In order to circumvent Bayesian filters and filters that block messages with only images, spammers enter 'normal' text at the bottom of the message in order to appear legitimate. Some spammers include this text in small font size.

**#8. Message subject contains email address or recipient name:** Either the complete email address or part of the email address (the part before the domain) is added to the subject in order to personalize the message and trick the recipient into thinking that it is a legitimate message. For legitimate mails there is no reason to enter the recipient's email address in the subject, so the presence of this is a pretty sure sign of spam.

**#7. Message body is base64 encoded:** Spammers use base64 to encode the message headers and body so that spam filters are not able to read the content and perform any filtering. Most email clients will decode the message so that the message can still be read by the recipient.

**#6. Sender address contains number or character sequence:** Spammers use automated programs to register thousands of email addresses. Since they are generated in bulk, they often include number or character sequences such as FRfJIrqOpV@hotmail.com or bob36189624@gmail.com. At first spammers used number sequences but when most spam filters started to block these types of addresses they changed to using character sequences which are harder to detect. (Patrol, The top 10 spam characteristics (#6-10) - Policy Patrol)

**#5. From: and Reply To: address are different:** This is a common feature of spam mails, but it is also very common with newsletters. The importance of this characteristic should be minimized since it is also found in legitimate emails.

**#4. Message body contains remote image:** In order to avoid spam messages from being blocked by word filters, spammers include an image in their message that cannot be filtered for words. In addition, upon opening the email message the image is downloaded from the spammer's website. Since each message contains a unique ID, the spammer will know exactly which recipient has viewed the mail. This indicates which email addresses are 'live' and can be sent even more spam.

**#3. Message contains only HTML body:** HTML messages usually include a plain text version of the email so that recipients with email clients that cannot read HTML can still view the message in plain text. However, many spammers tend to send HTML messages without this plain text body part. This is done to save on size and to force recipients to read the HTML version which automatically opens an image and connects to a web site when the message is opened. Newsletters also tend to send messages without a plain text body part, so it is important to use a white list of allowed newsletters so as not to catch any false positives.

**#2. Message contains many or only tags:** Some spammers try to circumvent content filters by placing lots of HTML comment tags within the email body text. In this way, content filters will not recognize the spam words since they are separated by comment tags. The recipient however, will not see the comment tags since these are not displayed when viewing the message in HTML. Therefore it is important to use an email filter that can filter emails by removing HTML tags first.

**#1. Recipient's email address is not in the To: or Cc: fields:** Red Earth Software found this to be the most commonly found characteristic in current spam messages. The reason for this is that the recipient's email address is hidden in the Bcc: field or X-receiver field, along with a substantial number of other email addresses. Spammers do this in order to conceal the fact that the mail was sent to a large number of recipients, and presumably so as not to publish their email list. Some persons might add recipients to the Bcc: field for sending out â€˜legitimateâ€™ mailings, but these will tend to be of a more personal nature (which you might wish to block anyway) since most professional companies do not use this method for sending newsletters or mailings. Note however that if you do block emails without a local recipient in the To: or Cc: field, you will be blocking all bcc: messages.

**Note :** Many spam filters check for the existence of these characteristics (and more) and use these to determine whether the message should be identified as spam. Some characteristics are strong indicators that a message is spam, others really cannot be taken into account at all since they can also exist in legitimate emails. A system checking for spam characteristics can be very effective, but must make use of a sophisticated scoring system in able to flag spam correctly, applying a different weight for each characteristic.

### 4.6 Understanding IP Addressing [082]

An IP address is an address used in order to uniquely identify a device on an IP network. The address is made up of 32 binary bits, which can be divisible into a network portion and host portion with the help of a subnet mask. The 32 binary bits are broken into four octets (1 octet = 8 bits). Each octet is converted to decimal and separated by a period (dot). For this reason, an IP address is said to be expressed in dotted decimal format (for example, 172.16.81.100). The value in each octet ranges from 0 to 255 decimal, or 00000000 - 11111111 binary.

Here is how binary octets convert to decimal: The right most bit, or least significant bit, of an octet holds a value of 20. The bit just to the left of that holds a value of 21. This continues until the left-most bit, or most significant bit, which holds a value of 27. So if all binary bits are a one, the decimal equivalent would be 255 as shown here:

1 1 1 1 1 1 1 1

128 64 32 16 8 4 2 1 (128+64+32+16+8+4+2+1=255)

Here is a sample octet conversion when not all of the bits are set to 1.

0 1 0 0 0 0 0 1

0 64 0 0 0 0 0 1 (0+64+0+0+0+0+0+1=65)

And this is sample shows an IP address represented in both binary and decimal.

10.    1.    23.    19 (decimal)

00001010.00000001.00010111.00010011 (binary)

These octets are broken down to provide an addressing scheme that can accommodate large and small networks. There are five different classes of networks, A to E. This document focuses on addressing classes A to C, since classes D and E are reserved and discussion of them is beyond the scope of this document.

**Note:** Also note that the terms "Class A, Class B" and so on are used in this document to help facilitate the understanding of IP addressing and subnetting. These terms are rarely used in the industry anymore because of the introduction of classless inter-domain routing (CIDR).

Given an IP address, its class can be determined from the three high-order bits. Following Figure 15 : IP Addressing Classes shows the significance in the three high order bits and the range of addresses that fall into each class. For informational purposes, Class D and Class E addresses are also shown.

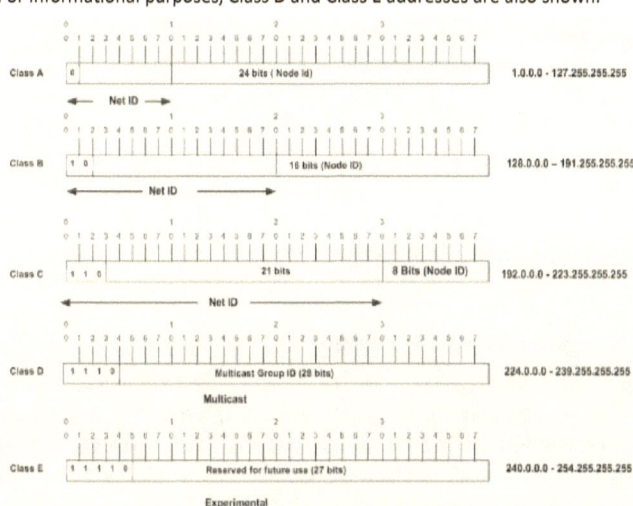

Figure 15 : IP Addressing Classes

71

### 4.7 MAC Address [083]

The Standards for Local Area Networks (LANs) generally comprise the physical layer, the medium access control (MAC) sublayer, and the logical link control (LLC) sublayer. In OSI terminology, the MAC and LLC sublayers are considered to be sublayers of the OSI Data Link layer. Both the MAC and LLC sublayers contain fields for addressing. A Universally Administered Address Block has been allocated for the assignment of Group MAC Addresses for use in Standards. This tutorial material contains a description of the MAC addressing conventions, the criteria that will be used when consideration for an assignment is made.

### 4.7.1 Binary and Hexadecimal Representation of LAN MAC Addresses

The Hexadecimal (in hexadecimal) Representation of LAN MAC addresses have been defined in ISO/IEC 10039 (LAN MAC Service Definition) and are used throughout this document.

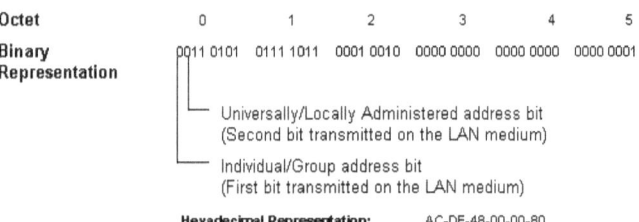

| Octet | 0 | 1 | 2 | 3 | 4 | 5 |
|---|---|---|---|---|---|---|
| Binary Representation | 0011 0101 | 0111 1011 | 0001 0010 | 0000 0000 | 0000 0000 | 0000 0001 |

Universally/Locally Administered address bit
(Second bit transmitted on the LAN medium)

Individual/Group address bit
(First bit transmitted on the LAN medium)

**Hexadecimal Representation:**      AC-DE-48-00-00-80

Figure 16 : Representation of LAN MAC Addresses

The 48-bit address (universal or local) is represented as a string of six octets. The octets are displayed from left to right, in the order that they are transmitted on the LAN medium, separated by hyphens. Each octet of the address is displayed as two hexadecimal digits. The bits within the octets are transmitted on the LAN medium from left to right. In the Binary Representation the first bit transmitted, of each octet, on the LAN medium is the least significant bit of that octet. The Individual/Group address bit is the least significant bit. The left-most bit of the Binary Representation

72

(Individual/Group address bit) of a MAC address distinguishes individual from group addresses. The Universally/Locally administered address bit is the next bit following the Individual/Group address bit. The U/L bit indicates whether the MAC address has been universally or locally assigned. For the previous example, the first octet transmitted is AC and the last octet transmitted is 80. The first bit transmitted is the low order bit of AC, a zero. The last bit transmitted is the high order bit of 80, a one.

# CHAPTER – 05

# ARCHITECTURE OF INTRUSION PREVENTATION SYSTEM

In this chapter, we are proposing the architecture of Intrusion Prevention System (IPS) to provide Network Security to the System. The proposed system should be responsive to monitor and detect the Network Attacks in Real Time. The system should raise an alert whenever it detects a Network Attack on the System. Such alerts should be stored in centralized database. The attackers IP and MAC Addresses should be stored in the centralized database in order to prevent similar future attacks.

## 5.1 DDoS Attack Mechanisms

The seriousness of the DDoS problem and the increased frequency of DDoS attacks have led to the advent of numerous DDoS defence mechanisms. Some of these mechanisms address a specific kind of DDoS attack such as attacks on Web servers or authentication servers. Other approaches attempt to solve the entire generic DDoS problem. Based on the activity level of DDoS defence mechanisms, we differentiate between preventive and reactive mechanisms.

## 5.1.1 DDoS Preventive Mechanisms

The goal of preventive mechanisms is either to eliminate the possibility of DDoS attacks altogether or to enable potential victims to endure the attack without denying services to legitimate clients. According to these goals we further divide preventive mechanisms into attack prevention and denial-of-service prevention mechanisms.

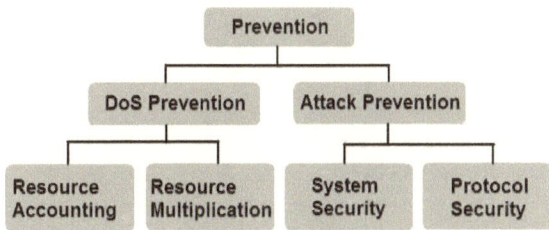

Figure 17 : DDoS Prevention Defence Mechanisms.

**We encourage you to consider the following options with respect to your needs:**

Implement router filters as described in [084]. This will lessen your exposure to certain denial-of-service attacks. Additionally, it will aid in preventing users on your network from effectively launching certain denial-of-service attacks.

If they are available for your system, install patches to guard against TCP SYN flooding as described in [085]. This will substantially reduce your exposure to these attacks but may not eliminate the risk entirely.

Disable any unused or unneeded network services. This can limit the ability of an intruder to take advantage of those services to execute a denial-of-service attack.

Enable quota systems on your operating system if they are available. For example, if your operating system supports disk quotas, enable them for all accounts, especially accounts that operate network services. In addition, if your operating system supports partitions or volumes (i.e., separately mounted file systems with independent attributes) consider partitioning your file system so as to separate critical functions from other activity.

Observe your system performance and establish baselines for ordinary activity. Use the baseline to gauge unusual levels of disk activity, CPU usage, or network traffic.

Routinely examine your physical security with respect to your current needs. Consider servers, routers, unattended terminals, network access points, wiring closets, environmental systems such as air and power, and other components of your system.

Use Tripwire or a similar tool to detect changes in configuration information or other files.

Invest in and maintain "hot spares" - machines that can be placed into service quickly in the event that a similar machine is disabled.

Invest in redundant and fault-tolerant network configurations.

Establish and maintain regular backup schedules and policies, particularly for important configuration information.

Establish and maintain appropriate password policies, especially access to highly privileged accounts such as UNIX root or Microsoft Windows NT Administrator. [086]

### 5.1.2 DDoS Detective Mechanisms

Reactive mechanisms strive to alleviate the impact of an attack on the victim. In order to attain this goal they need to detect the attack and respond to it. The goal of attack detection is to detect every attempted DDoS attack as early as possible and to have a low degree of false positives. Upon attack detection, steps can be taken to characterize the packets belonging to the attack stream and provide this characterization to the response mechanism [087] [088].

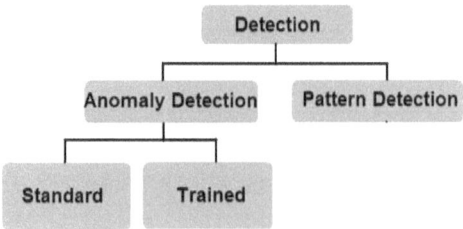

Figure 18: DDoS Detection Defence Mechanisms.

### 5.1.3 DDoS Mitigation Mechanisms

When a customer or the network infrastructure is under attack, monitoring is important for quick identification of the attack characteristics and entry points but the next question that immediately follows is, "What are you going to do to stop it?" Good mitigation techniques are a required part of a service provider's security architecture.

### 5.1.3.1 ACLs/Rate Limiting

Access control lists (ACL) or firewall filters are the first line of defence for a service provider. For a simple DDoS attack directed at a single customer, deployment of an egress ACL on the customer's edge router is an easy way to stop the attack. The problem with this technique is scaling both from a router performance perspective and as the number of attacks managed increases.

Operation personnel deploying the ACLs must know the performance limitation of the routers they are using. ASIC based ACLs will perform better than ACLs processed in software. Different ASICs can and do have different performance characteristics based on the packet size, interface speed and other features turned on in the router and interface cards. Most service providers have home grown scripts for their router configuration and ACL management.

Traffic loads must be monitored as the ACLs are removed to ensure that worm traffic from unpatched customers does not have a significant impact on other customers or the provider's backbone. Legitimate customer traffic may also be blocked by the ACLs and support organizations must be notified and prepared to answer customer's questions and complaints.

### 5.1.3.2 Destination based Black Hole Filtering

Black hole filtering is an effective, quick and simple technique for dropping attack traffic destined toward a victim. Using iBGP as a trigger mechanism, black hole filtering can be remotely triggered across the entire perimeter of a provider's network. This technique is used when more harm is done by the attack filling up a customer's circuit than by the loss of an individual site. Many times, traffic can be redirected to a different IP address through DNS.

Several variations of remotely triggered black hole filtering can be setup. By using different community strings, remote triggers can be setup for different types of routers such as edge and border. Community strings can be setup for different geographic regions or POPs in a provider's network. This flexibility allows the provider to identify the ingress points of the attack and only block traffic at those locations.

### 5.1.3.3 Attack Distribution and/or Isolation – Anycast

IPv4 anycast implementations have been in use on the Internet for at least the past 10 years. Particularly suited for single response UDP queries, DNS anycast architectures are in use in most tier 1 Internet providers' backbones. Anycast implementations can be used for both DNS authoritative and recursive implementations. Several root name servers are implementing anycast architectures to mitigate DDoS attacks [089]. Black hole filtering is a specialized form of anycast. Sinkholes can use anycast to distribute the load of an attack across many locations [090].

Many DNS anycast implementations are done using eBGP announcements. Anycast networks can be contained in a single AS or spam multiple AS's across the globe. Anycast provides two distinct advantages in regard to DoS/DDoS attacks. In a DoS attack, anycast localizes the effect of the attack. In a DDoS attack, the attack is distributed over a much larger number of servers, distributing the load of the attack and allowing the service to better withstand it.

### 5.1.3.4 Shell Script for SYN DDoS Attack

SYN Deflate is a tool designed by Solid Shell Security [091] to help stop and drop DDoS attacks on a server. The tool is fully automated and will help drop all types of SYN attacks. Once installed the CRON job will run and monitor all incoming connections and if an IP is attacking, that IP will be blocked and banned.

The options/flags available with this tool are as follows :

Tool Name :    ./synd_install.sh

-h --help ? : Display help information

-e --email email : Set e-mail used to send alerts

-c --conn ## : Number of connections to be considered a bad connection (default 30)

-b --ban <1,0> : Use CSF<1> or IPTables<0> to ban IPs (Default IPTables)

-t --time #### : How long should IPs remain banned?

-v --verbose : Turn on verbose mode to display all information (not implemented yet)

-d --debug : Turn on debug mode (not implemented yet)

### 5.2  WinPcap – example of an Intrusion Prevention System

WinPcap [092] is a free, public system for direct network access on Windows operating systems. Most applications access the network through widely used system primitives, like sockets. By using sockets, operating system copes with low level details (protocol handling, flow reassembly, etc.). WinPcap provides access to raw network data without protocol handling, or flow reassembly.

**The purpose of WinPcap is to provide direct network access to Windows applications; it provides facilities to:**

Capture raw packets, both the ones destined to the machine where it's running and the ones exchanged by other hosts (on shared media), filter packets according to user-specified rules before dispatching them to the application, transmit raw packets to the network, gather statistical values on the network traffic.

This set of capabilities is obtained by means of a device driver, and a couple of DLLs. WinPcap architecture includes a kernel-level packet filter, a low-level dynamic link library (packet.dll), and a high-level and system-independent library (wpcap.dll). Following figure shows the components of WinPcap architecture:

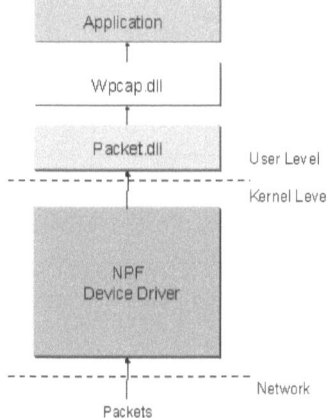

Figure 19 : Components of WinPcap architecture [092]

First, a capture system needs to bypass the protocol stack in order to access the raw data transiting on the network. This requires a portion running inside the kernel of operating system, interacting directly with the network interface drivers. This portion is much system dependent, and in WinPcap it is conceived as a device driver; called Netgroup Packet Filter (NPF), and currently different versions of the driver for Windows 95, Windows 98, Windows ME, Windows NT 4, Windows 2000 and Windows XP are provided. These drivers offer both basic features like packet capture and injection, as well as more advanced ones like a programmable filtering system and a monitoring engine. Thus, it can be used to restrict a capture session to a subset of the network traffic (e.g. it is possible to capture only the FTP traffic generated by a particular host), and the monitoring engine provides a powerful but simple to use mechanism to obtain statistics on the traffic (e.g. it is possible to obtain the network load or the amount of data exchanged between two hosts).

Second, the capture system must export an interface that user-level applications will use to take advantage of the features provided by the kernel driver. WinPcap provides two different libraries: packet.dll and wpcap.dll. The first one offers a low-level API that can be used to directly access the functions of the driver, with a programming interface independent from the Microsoft operating system. The second one exports a more powerful, system independent set of high level capture functions that are compatible with libpcap [093], the well known Unix capture library [092]. These functions allow capturing packets in a way independent from the underlying network hardware and operating system. Besides that, libpcap [093] compatibility allows writing portable network tools that will work on the whole Windows operating system family and on all the major Unix flavors. One major example of this kind of programs is Snort [094].

### 5.3 Snort – another example of an Intrusion Prevention System

Snort® [094] is an open source network intrusion prevention and detection system (IDS/IPS) developed by Sourcefire. Combining the benefits of signature, protocol, and anomaly-based inspection, Snort is the most widely deployed IDS/IPS technology worldwide. With millions of downloads and nearly 400,000 registered users, Snort has become the de facto standard for IPS.

Snort has modular plug-in architecture. There are three types of plug-in available in Snort: detection plug-ins, preprocessors, output plug-ins. Detection plug-ins check a single aspect of a packet for a value defined within a rule and determine if the packet data meets their acceptance criteria. For example, the TCP flags detection plug-in checks the flags section of TCP packets for matches with flag combinations defined in a particular rule. Detection plug-ins may be called multiple times per packet with different arguments.

Preprocessors are only called a single time per packet and may perform highly complex functions like port scan detection, TCP stream reassembly, IP defragmentation, http request normalization, or Telnet decode. They can directly manipulate packet data and even call the detection engine directly with their modified data. They can perform less complex tasks like statistics gathering or threshold monitoring as well.

Output plug-in's are also called once per packet after the preprocessor and detection engine. They provides real-time alerting capability, incorporating alerting mechanisms for syslog, user specified files, or a UNIX socket. They also provide logging of packets in many formats, including tcpdump [093] binary format or decoded ASCII format to a hierarchical set of directories that are named based on the IP address of the remote host. Database or XML logging plug-ins exists, as well.

Snort has three primary functional modes: sniffer, packet logger, and network intrusion detection system. Sniffer mode simply reads the packets off of the network and displays them for you in a continuous stream on the console. Packet logger mode logs the packets to the disk. Network intrusion detection mode is the most complex and configurable configuration, allowing Snort to analyze network traffic for matches against a user defined rule set, and perform several actions based upon what it sees.

The rules contain the information that defines the who, where, and what of a packet, as well as what to do in the event that a packet with all the attributes indicated in the rule should show up. The first item in a rule is the rule action. The rule action tells Snort what to do when it finds a packet that matches the rule criteria. There are five available default actions in Snort: alert, log, pass, activate, and dynamic.

alert - generate an alert using the selected alert method, and then log the packet,

log - log the packet,

pass - ignore the packet,

activate - alert and then turn on another dynamic rule,

dynamic - remain idle until activated by an activate rule , then act as a log rule.

One can also define his own rule types and associate one or more output plug-ins with them. He can then use the rule types as actions in Snort rules.

Snort is developed with the performance, simplicity, and flexibility in mind. Snort is logically divided into multiple components. These components work together to detect various attacks and to generate output in a required format. These components ride on top of the libpcap [093] or WinPcap [092] promiscuous packet capturing library, which provides a portable packet sniffing and filtering capability. Snort consists of the following major components [095]:

- ❖ Packet Decoder
- ❖ Preprocessors
- ❖ Detection Engine
- ❖ Logging and Alerting System
- ❖ Output Modules

Following figure shows the arrangement of these components. Any data packet coming from the network enters the packet decoder. And on its way towards the output modules, it is either dropped, logged or an alert is generated.

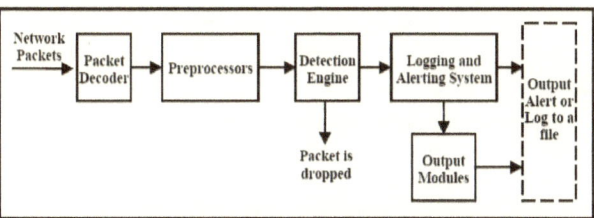

Figure 20 : Components of Snort [095]

### 5.3.1 Packet Decoder

The packet decoder takes packets from different types of network interfaces and prepares the packets to be preprocessed or to be sent to the detection engine. The interfaces may be Ethernet, SLIP, PPP, WiFi and so on [095]. It parses the packet and decodes the string of bytes into a packet structure that is formed of protocol fields and flags. Each subroutine in the decoder imposes order on the packet data by overlaying data structures on the raw network traffic. These decoding routines are called in order through the protocol stack, from the data link layer up through the transport layer, finally ending at the application layer. During this decoding process, it

83

validates the length and checksum fields. It then forwards the valid packets to the preprocessors.

### 5.3.2   Preprocessors

When a packet is received by Snort [094], it may not be ready for processing by the main Snort detection engine and application of Snort rules.

For example, a packet may be fragmented. Before searching a string within the packet or determine its exact size, defragmentation is required by assembling all fragments of the data packet. On IDS, before applying any rules or try to find a signature, the packets have to be reassembled [095]. The job of a preprocessor is to make a packet suitable for the detection engine to apply different rules to it. In addition, some preprocessors are used for other tasks such as detection of anomalies and obvious errors in data packets, decoding of HTTP URI. All enabled preprocessors operate on each packet. There is no way to bypass some of the preprocessors based upon some criteria.

### 5.3.3   The Detection Engine

The detection engine is the most important part of Snort [094]. Its responsibility is to detect if any intrusion activity exists in a packet. The detection engine employs Snort rules for this purpose. The rules are read into internal data structures or chains where they are matched against all packets. Snort organizes parts of packets to make the job of matching rules against them faster. It maintains detection rules in a two dimensional linked list of what are termed Chain Headers and Chain Options. The commonalities are condensed into a single Chain Header and individual detection signatures are kept in Chain Option structures. If a packet matches any rule, appropriate action is taken; otherwise the packet is dropped. Appropriate actions may be logging the packet or generating alerts.

### 5.3.4   Logging and Alerting System

This system is responsible from the generation of alerts and logging of packets and messages. Depending upon what the detection engine finds inside a packet, the packet may be used to log the activity or generate an alert. All of the log files are stored under a preconfigured location by default. This location can be configured using command line options. There are many command line options to modify the type and detail of information that is logged by the logging and alerting system.

### 5.3.5 Output Modules

Basically, these modules control the type of output generated by the logging and alerting system. Depending on the configuration, output modules can send output messages a number of other destinations. Commonly used output modules are:

The database module is used to store Snort output data in databases, such as MySQL, MSSQL or Oracle,

The SNMP module can be used to send Snort alerts in the form of traps to a management server,

The Sending Server Message Block (SMB) alerts module can send alerts to Microsoft Windows machines in the form of pop-up SMB alert windows,

The syslog module logs messages to the syslog utility (using this module you can log messages to a centralized logging server.),

XML or CSV modules can be used to save data in XML or comma separated files. The CSV files can then be imported into databases or spreadsheet software for further processing or analysis.

### 5.3.6 Snort_inline

Snort_inline [096] is basically a modified version of Snort [094]. It accepts packets from iptables [097], instead of libpcap [093]. It then uses new rule types to tell iptables if the packet should be dropped or allowed to pass based on the Snort rule set. You can think of Snort_inline as a NIPS that uses existing IDS signatures to make decisions on packets that traverse Snort_inline. Snort_inline is also an open source project like Snort. It is actually Snort itself with an addition, inline operation capability. It is being developed for Unix platforms and no Windows version exists at the time this thesis is being written. When it is operating in inline mode, it accepts packets from iptables, and then forwards them to the packet decoder after converting them to libpcap packet format. The packet flows toward the logging and alerting system as it is in the Snort architecture. In the logging and alerting subsystem, the appropriate output module for the matching rule is called. Unlike Snort, there are three additional rule types in Snort_inline:

❖ **drop** - The drop rule type will tell iptables to drop the packet and log it via usual Snort means,

❖ **reject** - The reject rule type will tell iptables to drop the packet, log it via usual Snort means, and send a TCP reset if the protocol is TCP or an ICMP port unreachable if the protocol is UDP,

❖ **sdrop** - The sdrop rule type will tell iptables to drop the packet. Nothing is logged.

Depending on the matching rule type, the packet is either forwarded using iptables, or dropped. Besides taking one of these actions, logging and/or alerting can also be done.

### 5.4  Cisco IOS IPS: Key Features and Benefits [098]:

Provides network-wide, distributed protection from many attacks, exploits, worms and viruses exploiting vulnerabilities in operating systems and applications.

Eliminates the need for a standalone IPS device at branch and telecommuter offices as well as small and medium-sized business networks.

Unique and risk rating based signature event action policy processor dramatically improves the ease of management of IPS policy.

Offers field-customizable worm and attack signature set and event actions

Offers inline inspection of traffic passing through any combination of router LAN and WAN interfaces in both directions.

Works with Cisco IOS® Firewall, control-plane policing, and other Cisco IOS Software security features to protect the router and networks behind the router.

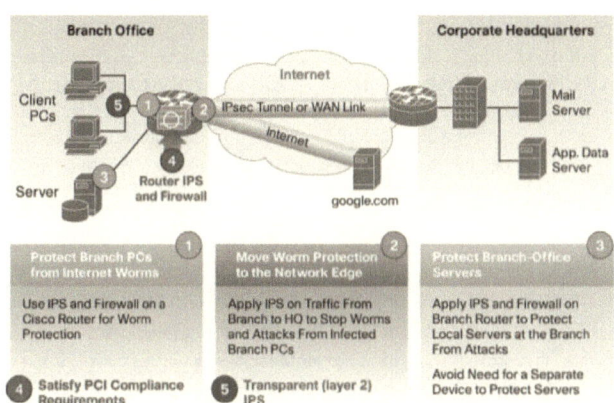

Figure 21: Cisco IOS Intrusion Prevention System

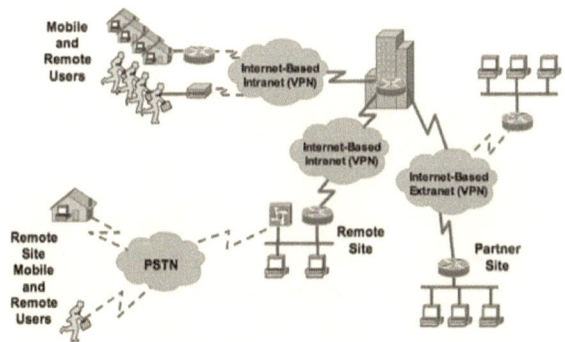

**Network using CISCO IPS**

Figure 22 : Network using CISCO Intrusion Prevention System

87

# CHAPTER – 06

# ARCHITECTURE OF SPAM CONTROL MECHANISMS

In this chapter, we are proposing the architecture of SPAM controlling mechanisms.

## 6.1 Spam Classifier

To make a Spam Filter, first we have to work on Spam classifier. Spam Classifier has to decide on the basis of previous information, rules, and spam sets that, if some Email is a SPAM or HAM (Non-Spam). This classification can be either Hard Classification or soft classification.

In Hard Classification, we made some rules to classify a Spam and then we fix this rule, once classified, the nature of Spam Email can not be altered. For eg. We have hard coded that any Mobile Number is of 10 digits, now in any circumstances, we will not accept an eleven digit mobile number as a genuine data.

In Soft Classification, we made some rules to classify a Spam and then if we find a data which is declared as Non-spam then our classifier will declare it as false positive. So we can alter the classification of Spam Email based on user inputs, for eg. If some club is sending same email to more than 200 recipients and it's classified by Spam Classifier as Spam Email since it sent to more than 100 recipients at a time, so it will be delivered in Spam Folder on the recipients. Suppose if any one recipient will check this email in spam folder and then mentioned it as Non-Spam by clicking some button, in this case Soft Classifier will report the sender and that Email as False positive, and now on all the emails from this sender will be treated as Ham. There will not be any input to permit false positive type from the administrator of Email server. Therefore this classifier technique will still be an automated process.

Let's assume that,

m  is a message which may be either spam or ham(not-spam)

M  is the universal set of messages.

M is partitioned into two sets, spam and non-spam.

such that,

every m ∈ M,

where, M = spam ∪ non-spam

and spam ∩ non-spam= Φ

An Ideal Spam Classifier should be a function :

is_spam : M ▣ { T, F}

such that,

is_spam (m) = T iff m ∈ M ,

It means that, if spam classifier is_spam( ) has found that message m is spam than m must belong to universal set of messages M.

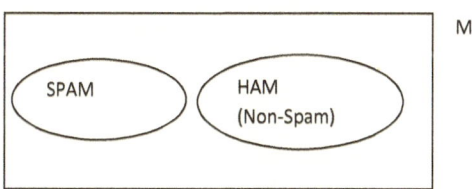

Now to make an ideal Spam Classifier is not possible because of the changing nature of Spam and growing intelligence of Spammers.

But if we can make a soft classifier WoW such that

WoW ( m ) ≈ is_spam( m )

Then it will be the great work. Let's try to make WoW ( ) classifier such that it can filter more than 80% of spam.

## 6.2 Whitelists

A Whitelist can be formed with sender's email id or IP addresses or MAC Addresses which are declared as false-positive by the Spam filter. Whitelist belongs to a legitimate list of users sending non-spam or genuine email messages. Your Address book on your email client is your white list as you may assume that these addresses will not send any spam email. Generally Spam Filters maintain their whitelist explicitly. Global Whitelists may be maintained by companies providing email services.

Even this whitelist can be compromised by the spammer as they use a real email address without the consent of legitimate user to spread spam. Many companies like Google are even selling the active and real email addresses. Malware and Adware can easily make this task positive.

### 6.3 Blacklists

A blacklist can be a list of senders email id's, URL's or IP addresses which have been reported as Spam in the past. Every organization is now making a blacklist of their own from their spam experience, so that Spam filters can easily detect the possible Spam. The organization may also rely on the BlackLists generated by other standard international research organizations. Some of these organizations are :

Domain Name System Blacklists, also known as DNSBL's or DNS Blacklists, are spam blocking lists. (www.dnsbl.info/)

The SpamCop Blocking List (SCBL) lists IP addresses which have transmitted reported email to SpamCop users. (www.spamcop.net/bl.shtml)

The Spamhaus Block List ("SBL") Advisory is a database of IP addresses from which Spamhaus does not recommend the acceptance of electronic mail. (www.spamhaus.org/sbl/)

Blacklist monitor, is a Spam blacklist (RBL, DNSBL) is a list of IP addresses and domain names that supposedly are source of email spam.

etc.

### 6.4 Collaborative Spam Filtering

In case of Collaborative spam Filtering, when a recipient receive a spam email, it reports the same to email server, which updates the spam/black list with following details: IP Address, Email Address, URL etc.

Whenever another recipient receive the email from black listed IP or URL or Email address, they have been informed by Email Server that this message is a possible spam. Generally such messages are transferred to Spam Email Box, if recipients find it genuine for him, they make Make It genuine by clicking some buton like "NOT SPAM".

This is a collaborative way of fighting spam, its success rates depends upon the number of users who have accessed the spam email before you. This is the reason why spammers are sending Millions of Spam Emails per second, so that by the time it's get reported as Spam, its payload should get transferred.

### 6.5 Greylisting

GreyListing is another type of listing IP Addresses, Email Id's, URL etc. where the Spam filter is not sure about the message, therefore they list them n GreyListing, so that another chance can be given to such source of messages. Once confirmed about the Spam nature of message, it does get transferred from Grey to Black Listing.

### 6.6 Spam Botnets

There are different categories of Spam botnets which are as follows :

### 6.6.1 Form filling bots:

These bots read the form served by the site, and mechanically fill data into the fields. These spam bots don't understand common field names (email, name, subject) their motive is to fill junk in all the fields, that's all. On my site, while there are some bots those look at the type of the field, in order to clear the client side validation and fill in data based on the type. Single-line edit controls (type=text) get name, email, and subject, while textareas get the comment body. Some bots will fill the same data into all the fields of the same type, while others will enter (for example) different first names into each of the single-line fields.

Form-filling bots can be stopped by including editable fields on the form that are invisible to people. These fields are called Honeypot and are validated when the form data is posted. If they contain any text, then the submitter must be a bot, and the submission is rejected.

Using randomized obscured field names, and strict validation can also stop these bots. If the email field must have an @-sign, and the name field must not, and the bot can't tell which field is email and which is name, then the chances it will make a successful post have been greatly reduced.

### 6.6.2 Playback Spambots

These are bots which have recorded POST data which they replay back to the form submission URL. A person visits the form the first time, and records the form data. Certain fields are marked as slots to be filled in with randomized spam later, but the structure of the form is played back verbatim each time. This includes the names of the fields, and the contents of hidden fields.

These bots don't even bother looking at the form as served by the site, but blindly post their canned data to the submission URL. Using unusual field names to avoid these bots will only work for a week or so, when they will then record the new field name, and begin posting with it.

A playback bot can be stopped by varying the hidden data on the form so that it will not be valid forever. A timestamp is a simple way to do this, making it possible to detect when old data is being replayed. The timestamp can be made tamper-proof by hashing it with a secret and including the hash in the hidden data of the form. Replaying can be further hindered by including the client's IP address in the hash, so that data can't even be immediately replayed across an army of spambots.

### 6.6.3 Trained Human as Bot

This is a very serious category of Spambots where they have used Human doing the spam. They can solve any type of CAPTCHA, they can pass any AI test to beat the security. By the time incentives will be there for spamming, this type of bots cannot be controlled.

Financial institutions have dealt with banking trojans for more than a decade and the number of trojans targeting online banking transactions has increased dramatically during this span. This increase represents a challenge to financial institutions and their customers.

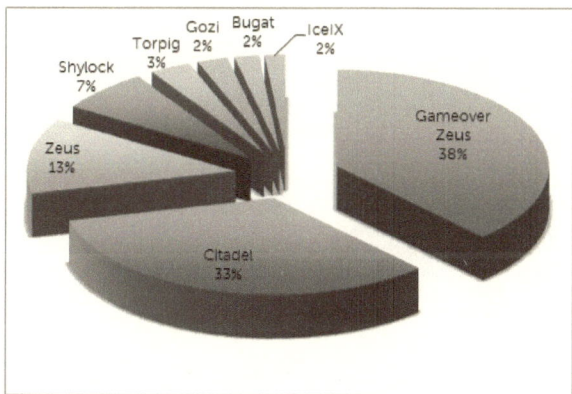

Figure 23: Percentage of banking malware by botnet in 2013. [099]

| THREAT | TARGETS | AVAILABILITY |
|--------|---------|--------------|
| Zeus | Targeted/Commodity | Public |
| IcelX | Targeted/Commodity | Public |
| Citadel | Targeted/Commodity | Public/Private |
| Gameover Zeus | Targeted/Commodity | Private |
| Shylock | Commodity | Private |
| Bugat | Commodity | Private |
| Gozi | Targeted/Commodity | Private |
| Torpig | Commodity | Private |

Table 1. Comparison of most active botnets observed in 2013 [099]

### 6.6.4 Zeus

The Zeus banking trojan (originally called PRG or Zbot) was first discovered by the CTU research team in 2007 after it was used in a credential-theft attack targeting the United States Department of Transportation. Since the Zeus 2.0.8.9 source code was stolen and leaked to the underground community in May 2011, nearly every banking trojan contains Zeus features. The relative maturity and broad success of Zeus has provided a model in the weaponization and development of other families of banking trojans.

The Zeus toolkit is made up of three parts: a builder, the actual Trojan horse malware, and a C2 web panel. The builder allows the attacker to edit and compile the configuration file and to build the actual trojan. The trojan is then delivered to the victim's system, where it modifies the compromised computer and steals information. The C2 server monitors and controls the trojan and stores stolen data.

CTU researchers have observed delivery of Zeus via many different infection vectors with emphasis on use of spam campaigns and exploit kits, techniques that leverage email and web browser technology to reach and install malware on end-user systems. Zeus uses port 80 (HTTP) for all of its communication between the victim's system and the C2 server. This port is typically not blocked or monitored for outbound connections. Table 3 lists the statistics for Zeus samples analyzed by CTU researchers in 2013.

| ATTRIBUTE | COUNT |
|---|---|
| C2 servers | 1,113 |
| Configuration files | 1,328 |
| Samples | 8,188 |
| Encryption keys | 542 |
| Versions | 14 |
| Targets | 740 (unique); 163,812 (total) |

Table 2. Zeus samples analyzed in 2013 [099]

### 6.6.5 Gameover Zeus (Zeus P2P)

Gameover is one of the most capable Zeus variants. It appeared in July 2011, shortly after the Zeus 2.x source code was leaked. It is typically distributed through high-volume spam campaigns that infect victims' systems via email attachments and URL redirects to drive-by download exploit kits. Ongoing development and operation of Gameover Zeus has been extremely focused and driven by a small group of threat actors who tightly control the feature set and offer services to a small, tightly controlled segment of the criminal economy. Table 6 lists the statistics for Gameover Zeus samples analyzed by CTU researchers in 2013.

| ATTRIBUTE | COUNT |
|---|---|
| Configuration files | 341 |
| Samples | 24,343 |
| Unique bot IDs | 150-175K (per day) |
| Unique IP addresses | 200-250K (per day) |
| Versions | 16 |
| Targets | 517 (unique); 31,200 (total) |

Table 3. Gameover Zeus samples analyzed in 2013.[099]

### 6.7 HoneyPot Trap

A HoneyPot is a trap programmed to detect spam attacks, sometimes to deflect the user to nonsense section of code, or to, counteract attempts at unauthorized use of potential system or system module. Mostly, a HoneyPot contains a workstation, some application data, or a website that pretends to be a part of system, but it is actually isolated and monitored, to engage the Spam bots to provided resources of value to attackers. Just like the police catching a criminal and then free undercover their surveillance to know about other criminals and their future activities.

As in attached Figure 24 : Honeypot Systems [100], Honeypots can be implemented inside or outside the firewall, they are basically the variants of an Intruder Detection Systems (IDS) but it focus more on information gathering and deception.

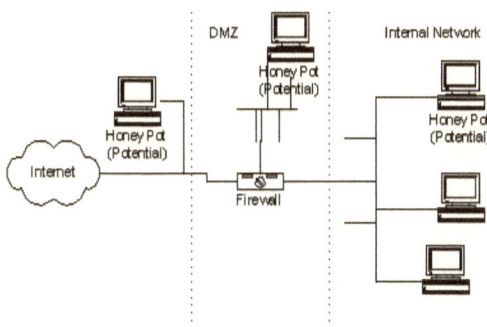

Figure 24 : Honeypot Systems

A Honey Pot system is setup to be easier prey for intruders than true production systems but with minor system modifications so that their activity can be logged of traced. The general thought is that once an intruder breaks into a system, they will come back for subsequent visits. During these subsequent visits, additional information can be gathered and additional attempts at file, security and system access on the Honey can be monitored and saved. [100]

**Generally, there are two popular reasons or goals behind setting up a Honey Pot [100]:**

Learn how intruders probe and attempt to gain access to your systems. The general idea is that since a record of the intruder's activities is kept, you can gain insight into attack methodologies to better protect your real production systems.

Gather forensic information required to aid in the apprehension or prosecution of intruders. This is the sort of information often needed to provide law enforcement officials with the details needed to prosecute.

97

The common line of thought in setting up Honey Pot systems is that it is acceptable to use lies or deception when dealing with intruders. What this means to you when setting up a Honey Pot is that certain goal have to be considered [100].

**Those goals are [100]:**

The Honey Pot system should appear as generic as possible. If you are deploying a Microsoft NT based system, it should appear to the potential intruder that the system has not been modified or they may disconnect before much information is collected.

You need to be careful in what traffic you allow the intruder to send back out to the Internet for you don't want to become a launch point for attacks against other entities on the Internet. (One of the reasons for installing a Honey Pot inside of the firewall!)

You will want to make your Honey Pot an interesting site by placing "Dummy" information or make it appear as though the intruder has found an "Intranet" server, etc. Expect to spend some time making your Honey Pot appear legitimate so that intruders will spend enough time investigating and perusing the system so that you are able to gather as much forensic information as possible.

The first caveat is the consideration that if the information gathered from a Honey Pot system is used for prosecution purposes, it may or may not be deemed admissible in court. While information regarding this issue is difficult to come by, having been hired as an expert witness for forensic data recovery purposes, I have serious reservations regarding whether or not all courts will accept this as evidence or if non-technical juries are able to understand the legitimacy of it as evidence[100].

The second main caveat for consideration is whether hacking organizations will rally against an organization that has set "traps" and make them a public target for other hackers. Examples of this sort of activity can be found easily on any of the popular hacker's sites or their publications[100].

### 6.7.1 Honey Pot Solutions

Implementation of a Honey Pot solution as part of a security system first involves the decision of whether to purchase a commercial solution or decide to develop your own [100].

### 6.7.2 Building a Honey Pot

There is a variety of public domain tools and software available that can be useful to help you setup a Honey Pot as well as many sites dedicated to helping guide you through the process. Most tools seem to have originated on the Unix platform, while many have been ported to Microsoft NT [100].

What you will need to create or develop your own Honey Pot system are a minimum of the following components and considerable configuration time [100]:

A Workstation or PC. It appears as though an Intel-based workstation is fine.

An operating system. I prefer BSD Unix or RedHat as there are more tools available for the Unix platform than NT.

Sniffer package.

### 6.7.3 Commercial Honey Pot Systems

There are a variety of commercial Honey Pot systems available. The operating systems most widely supported are Microsoft NT and Unix[100].

**Some of the commercial Honey Pot systems available are:**

- ❖ Network Associates, Cybercop Sting
- ❖ Tripwire, Tripwire
- ❖ Fred Cohen and Associates, Deception Toolkit
- ❖ Recourse Technologies, ManTrap

Honeypot fields are invisible fields on the form. Invisible is different than hidden. Hidden is a type of field that is not displayed for editing. Bots understand hidden fields, because hidden fields often carry identifying information that has to be returned intact. Invisible fields are ordinary editable fields that have been made invisible in the browser.

The invisibility of the honeypot fields is a key way that bots reveal themselves. Because bots do not process the entirety of the HTML, CSS, and Javascript in the form, and because they do not build a visual representation of the page, and because they do not perceive the form as people do, they cannot distinguish invisible fields from visible ones. They will put data into honeypot fields because they don't know any better.

**The form is built as usual, including:**

editable fields for all of the information we want to collect from the user,

hidden fields for identifying information, including the timestamp, the spinner, and the entry id,

invisible honeypot fields of all types, including submission buttons.

# CHAPTER – 07

# PROPOSED NETWORK INTRUSION PREVENTION
# SYSTEM

## 7.1 Research Methodology

The way in which research is conducted may be conceived of in terms of the research philosophy subscribed to, the research strategy employed and so the research instruments utilized (and perhaps developed) in the pursuit of a goal – the research objective(s) - and the quest for the solution of a problem - the research question. The purpose of this section is to:

Discuss our research philosophy in relation to other philosophies;

Expound our research strategy, including the research methodologies adopted;

Introduce the research instruments that we have developed and utilized in the pursuit of our goals.

This section details out the research methodology for the present study. It explains the research objectives and a suitable methodology to achieve those objectives. The objectives of this study were to identify and propose a solution for Intrusion Prevention Mechanism to avoid SPAM attacks through Spam-bots.. This involved an exhaustive study of the classification of DDoS attacks, different strategies to prevent Intrusion, different Intrusion Prevention systems available in the market and details of the results of new proposed Intrusion Prevention System. In addition the study also assessed the impact of Spam-bots over the online network applications. This was followed by proposing a model validation through case studies involving post-mortem analysis of the available systems. The research methodology has to be robust in order to minimize errors in data collection and analysis. Owing to this, various methodologies namely interview (telephonic, structured and unstructured) and case study were chosen for data collection. This section describes the pilot study, participants of the study, instrumentation done for the study, data collection, and data analysis procedures of the entire study.

### 7.1.1 Pilot Study

The pilot study formed the pedestal for the research. It was conducted on various IT professionals and IT students working in various software companies and professional colleges. They were asked to list down the various risks that they have faced during the Internet Use while executing their routine jobs. Through, the pilot survey, a list of specific risk items were identified and used for the study. Furthermore, these professionals were also asked to identify and rate the available Intrusion Prevention systems available in the market. Based on the findings of this pilot study, the problem statement was designed.

### 7.1.2 Research Strategies

In the following Table, we list the methodologies identified by Galliers (1991, p.149), indicating whether they typically conform to the positivist or interpretivist paradigms.

| Scientific/Positivist | Used | Interpretivist/Anti-positivist | Used |
|---|---|---|---|
| Laboratory Experiments | √ | Subjective/ Argumentative | √ |
| Field Experiments | √ | Reviews | |
| Surveys | | Action Research | √ |
| Case Studies | √ | Case Studies | √ |
| Theorem Proof | | Descriptive/Interpretive | |
| Forecasting | | Futures Research | |
| Simulation | √ | Role/Game Playing | |

Laboratory experiments permit the researcher to identify precise relationships between a small numbers of variables that are studied

102

intensively via a designed laboratory situation using quantitative analytical techniques with a view to making generalisable statements applicable to real-life situations. The key weakness of laboratory experiments is the "limited extent to which identified relationships exist in the real world due to over simplification of the experimental situation and the isolation of such situations from most of the variables that are found in the real world". (Galliers, 1991, p.150).

Field experiments extend laboratory experiments into real organisations and their real life situations, thereby achieving greater realism and diminishing the extent to which situations can be criticised as contrived. In practice it is difficult to identify organisations that are prepared to be experimented on and still more difficult to achieve sufficient control to make replication viable.

Case studies involve an attempt to describe relationships that exist in reality, very often in a single organisation. Case studies may be positivist or interpretivist in nature, depending on the approach of the researcher, the data collected and the analytical techniques employed. Reality can be captured in greater detail by an observer-researcher, with the analysis of more variables than is typically possible in experimental and survey research. Case studies can be considered weak as they are typically restricted to a single organisation and it is difficult to generalise findings since it is hard to find similar cases with similar data that can be analysed in a statistically meaningful way. Furthermore, different researchers may have different interpretations of the same data, thus adding research bias into the equation.

Simulation involves copying the behaviour of a system. Simulation is used in situations where it would be difficult normally to solve problems analytically and typically involves the introduction of random variables. As with experimental forms of research, it is difficult to make a simulation sufficiently realistic so that it resembles real world events.

Subjective/argumentative research, for example hermeneutics and phenomenology) requires the researcher to adopt a creative or speculative stance rather than act as an observer. It is a useful technique since new theories can be built, new ideas generated and subsequently tested. However, as an unstructured and subjective form of research, there is a strong chance of researcher bias.

Action research is a form of applied research where the researcher attempts to develop results or a solution that is of practical value to the people with whom the research is working, and at the same time developing theoretical knowledge. Through direct intervention in problems, the researcher aims to create practical, often emancipatory, outcomes while also aiming to re-inform existing theory in the domain studied. As with case studies, action research is usually restricted to a single organisation making it difficult to generalise findings, while different researchers may interpret events differently. The personal ethics of the researcher are critical, since the opportunity for direct researcher intervention is always present.

### 7.1.3 RESEARCH DESIGN

The exploratory and descriptive research design was adopted due to the nature of the study. Exploratory research provides insights into and comprehension of an issue or situation. Exploratory research is a type of research conducted because a problem has not been clearly defined. Exploratory research helps to determine the best research design, data collection method and selection of subjects. While descriptive research, also known as statistical research, describes data and characteristics about the population or phenomenon being studied. Descriptive research answers the questions who, what, where, when and how.

**Research Question 1:** What are the specific risk factors that impact the success and performance of the research output?

We have collected the data through different Spam and Network Attacks reports, that what is the intensity of such Network Intrusion attacks, what are the cost involved in sending such Spam's through botnets; through these different online reports published by leading Network research organizations and companies providing Anti-Network Intrusion software tools.

In order to validate the results and assess them in light of primary data, the further analysis was carried out.

**Research Question 2:** How much do these risk dimensions vary across the demographics and project characteristics?

In order to study how these dimensions of risk vary across the personal and project characteristics, we have tested the primary data. This test revealed how these dimensions diverge in case of different levels of designation, experience and age. We have noticed that the risk dimensions deviate among the different team sizes, duration of the project and the total value of the project. The Internet savvy persons are using different shortcuts and applications to fill up the online data quickly like using browser cache and other useful tools like RoboForm etc.

**Research Question 3:** How can preventing Spam will reduce the amount of Network Intrusion?

We have studied through various case studies and published reports of Intrusion Prevention Companies that Spammers or Intruders are preparing botnets in order to create spam on web, for this purpose they are attacking the network machines with virus/worms/Trojans etc to gain the access of machines. To create Spam is the major objective of intruders, for which we need a Modern Network Intrusion Prevention system. We have tested the primary data generated by collecting intrusion threats from different users.

The test reports have revealed that in different countries with different level of IT literacy, and awareness of such DDoS and other Intrusion attacks, different precautions have bbeen considered. Google Inc. have presented Google ReCAPTCHA tool to authenticate the existence of User and accepted worldwide in order to prevent DDoS attacks and to detect a Botnet, but we have seen alternatives solutions to fool ReCAPTCHA.

**Research Question 4 :** Can we restrict Spammers by using some other Software trick to prevent Web Spam ?

I have studied that Spammers are learning the anti-doses to security measures in no time. By the time we produce a new software solutions the spammers make a trick to spoof our solution. So we think that we have to hit their financial structure, one which is funding the Spam servers and Spam professionals. We strongly recommend using the behavioral solutions to prevent the spam.

We have used Honeypots in a different manner to restrict the Spamming. We are not giving any message to the Spammers that their access is restricted or they IP has been blocked, but our proposed system is using some artificial intelligent rules to differentiate between valid users and spambots and making black list, white list and grey list.

### 7.1.4 Formulation of Hypothesis

For testing purpose, above research questions were converted into hypotheses. The dimensions of risk and organization's environment were used for forming the corresponding hypotheses, each addressing the overall success and the performance constructs. The demographic characteristics and organizational climate dimensions were also used for forming the hypothesis relating to the various risk dimensions identified using factor analysis. The hypothesis for testing the relation of the organizational climate dimensions and demographic characteristics with software risk dimensions is as follows:

**Null Hypothesis (H0):** By minimizing the amount of Spam generated there will be no effect on the Intrusion Prevention, proposed solution will not be able to reduce Spam.

**H1:** Spam is a type of Intrusion. The proposed solution will minimize the Spam and accordingly help to stop Intrusion in critical network applications, and will play a key role to make an Intrusion Prevention System.

### 7.1.5 Introduction to Proposed Solution

After studying the pros and cons of several of Intrusion Prevention Systems, in this chapter we are proposing a new Intrusion Prevention System. We have considered all the advantages, tried to remove the major disadvantages given by different IPS's as on date. We have noticed that the authentication check is always checked by Login_id and Password mechanism which is quite vulnerable. We have proposed a Centralized online system to deal with global vulnerabilities activities due to Intrusion.

We have introduced a new concept of M=Key in which the IPS clients will be having a unique Application Identification i.e. App_Id, which will be combined with MAC address and IP Address of the network clients.

We have seen that in online applications, the authentication mechanism is changing day by day from passwords to one-time-passwords as SMS or Email to RFID kits to biometric authentication. The authentication mechanism is changing every day, but the Attackers are also learning the same skills and updating themselves and therefore developing new techniques for DDoS attacks. Even CAPTCHA have failed to identify that if some human is interacting with the system or some bot is there. New concept of CAPTCHA trading is popular these days, which is providing plug-in for all the popular open source browsers like Mozilla Firefox, etc. There CAPTCHA trading plug-ins are able to crack the CAPTCHA challenges coming on the websites or at the authentication points in a System. Some of the examples are : Death by Captcha, Captcha Trader Mipony Plugin, Tumblr Captcha Trader, Paresseux, etc. Now even after many updation's Google ReCaptcha becomes easily vulnerable.

When all the IT Tech's were working on proving a more secure and novel ideas for User Authentication techniques, we have worked differently. We have tried to hit on the financial model of the attackers; We have tried to find out the main purpose because of which attackers are doing Intrusion in our Critical Online Applications. We have worked on a hypothesis that,

What will happen if Attackers comes in financial loss even after doing intrusion ?

What will happen if Attackers are allowed to do 95% less Intrusion in a day ?

What will happen if different Online Web Services starts sharing there list of Intruders in real time?

What will happen if we work together to Stop Network Intrusion ?

In this research we have implemented some techniques which hits on the financial models or Intruders/Spammers. As lots of attackers are doing DDoS attacks on vulnerable network machines with little or no security precautions. These machines are hacked or compromised to make a Zombie's to create and propagate Spam. When similar techniques will be implemented on other domains, we are sure that Intrusion will be minimized and accordingly Intruders/Spammers will come in the financial losses.

## 7.2 Requirements for Proposed Intrusion Prevention System

The major Functional Requirements for an Intrusion Prevention System need to be discussed before the mechanisms of security architecture. The Functional requirements of an IPS are outlined below:

**Online operations:** In order to perform real time protection, an IPS must operate in online mode at crucial points of the network. IPS can take the required action immediately only when they operate online, discarding any suspicious packets before they reach their target and blocking the remainder flow from that source.

**High performance:** Packet processing must be at the real time traffic speed. Poor performance of IPS will result in slow network speed and lost of packets. Thus, an IPS should perform analysis at very high data rates; degradation in network performance is not at all acceptable.

**Scalability:** An IPS deployment should be scalable in performance and management. IPS could be deployed to medium and large networks without significant performance degradation. NIPS deployment should also provide scalable management for multiple Sensors deployed at choke points of the network.

**Reliability and availability:** Fail of an online device will directly affect the network up-time. Since IPS's are installed on crucial points where any failure can cause the lost of a vital network path and again, can lead to a DDoS condition. Thus, an extremely low failure rate is very important in order to maximize the network up-time and as an assurance, the device should support fail-over to another IPS operating in a fail-over group or provide fail-open option [101]. It is also important that rebooting of online devices will turn into network downtime for the duration of reboot.

**Detection accuracy:** An IPS must detect attacks and should not block the valid traffic flow. Since IPS's operate online, false positives can lead to a DDoS condition and become a new tool for attackers. The user must be able to trust that the IPS is blocking only the malicious traffic [101]. NIPS should not block the valid traffic and prevent employees doing their jobs.

**Ability to perform various types of detection analysis:** IPS's are only as valuable as their detection engines. Success or failure of an IPS depends mainly on its detection engine. There are various detection methods that are used in existing IDS's; each has success at detecting different types of intrusions. Mixing these various methods to use their superior parts and eliminating their weak points can form out a system that is more reliable than any of these methods alone. This would result in less false positives which are the main problem of existing IDSs.

**Low latency:** Since IPS is operating online and all traffic has to flow through them, the latency on these devices affects the network performance. Packets should be processed quickly enough that end nodes cannot sense the performance degradation. The overall latency of IPS must be as minimal as the latency of other online devices such as firewalls, router, and load balancers.

**Easier management:** An IPS allows the security managers to choose the response they want among various response mechanisms. Since IPSs are not only detecting attacks, but also preventing them by limiting or blocking which directly affects the network performance. Thus, configuring an IPS is a complex job. It is important to make the security managers' job of configuration as easy and simple as possible by providing them a user friendly interface to set and change configuration and eliminate the dreadful results of configuration errors [102].

**Safety of historic data:** Beyond detecting and preventing attacks, IPS should save the evidence of an intrusion for historical analysis. In order to do this, historic data could be copied for safe and offline observation. Mechanisms for the safety of these data should be in place.

109

**Data analysis capability:** IPS should be having a mechanism to allow security managers access individual packets from summary reports, to minimize administration efforts.

**Patch Update:** IPS needs to be updated time to time with patches in order to update with new DDoS attacks, detection and mitigation policies.

Modular Design: IPS needs to be made using modular design in order to easily upgrade new functionalities and mechanisms.

### 7.3 Desired Goals for proposed IPS Architecture

In our case the proposed Intrusion Prevention System will be working on an IPS Server in a distributed Client Server architecture. When you design such a client/server application, you're balancing several sets of requirements. You want to build the fastest, most productive application for your users. You also want to ensure the integrity of application data, make the most of existing hardware investments, and build in scalability for the future. In addition, as a Visual FoxPro developer, you want to make the development process as streamlined and cost-efficient as possible. [103]

**To be a truly reliable Intrusion Prevention System, following are the design goals for such a system:**

**Fault-Tolerant:** It can recover from component failures without performing incorrect actions.

**Highly Available:** It can restore operations, permitting it to resume providing services even when some components have failed.

**Recoverable:** Failed components can restart themselves and rejoin the system, after the cause of failure has been repaired.

**Consistent:** The system can coordinate actions by multiple components often in the presence of concurrency and failure. This underlies the ability of a distributed system to act like a non-distributed system.

**Scalable:** It can operate correctly even as some aspect of the system is scaled to a larger size. For example, we might increase the size of the network on which the system is running. This increases the frequency of network outages and could degrade a "non-scalable" system. Similarly, we might increase the number of users or servers, or overall load on the system. In a scalable system, this should not have a significant effect.

**Predictable Performance:** The ability to provide desired responsiveness in a timely manner.

**Secure:** The system authenticates access to data and services [103]

Distributed Architecture: The monitoring agents can be deployed at multiple penetration points within a network.

**Centralized Control:** The server will be placed centrally in our Client/Server model so that all the monitoring agents can be controlled and monitored centrally and independently. We can schedule and synchronize each monitoring agent and can also apply different configuration policies at required monitors.

**Heterogeneous Environment:** The proposed system will be independent of used Operating System. It should work will most common Operating Systems available.

**Graceful Degradation:** Failure of one component will not down the entire system, some functionality may reduce but System should recover in no time.

These are high standards, which are challenging to achieve. Probably the most difficult challenge is a distributed system must be able to continue operating correctly even when components fail.

The IPS at client end is used to monitor the events which are involved in network security attacks. The IPS is also required to check the attack patterns as per the knowledgebase maintained in the centralized database of IPS. The IPS knowledgebase need to be updated time to time to grow with new network security attack type, its prevention, detection and mitigation policies with the changing trends.

### 7.4 Major strengths of proposed intrusion prevention system are:

- ❖ Automatically Identifies and Blocks Threats
- ❖ Reduces Time Spent Reviewing Log Files to Identify Threats
- ❖ Reduces Need for Manpower to Monitor Threats
- ❖ Enhances Network Security Architecture

### 7.5 Architecture of Proposed IPS

| Tier – 1 | Tier - 2 | Tier – 3 |
|---|---|---|
| Graphical User Interface | Intrusion Prevention System Centralized Server | IPS Clients |

Figure 25 : Proposed IPS Multi-Tier Architecture

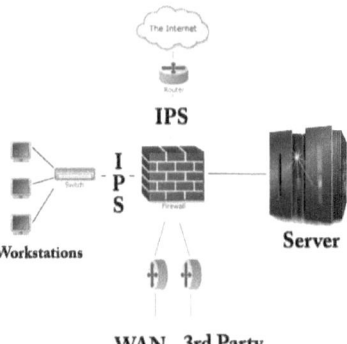

Figure 26 : Proposed IPS System Block Diagram

The proposed Intrusion Prevention System will be Three-tier architecture. A Graphical User Interface will be on Tier-1, Intrusion Prevention System will be on Tier-2 as a centralized server, IPS Clients will be there on Tier-3 distributed over network.

### 7.5.1 Tier-1 Graphical User Interface of IPS

A graphical user interface is required to interact with the IPS. This Web-based User Interface can be used remotely and can analyse the information stored on the IPS Server. Through this User Interface we can manage security policies, digital signatures and requests coming by IPS clients. All the user interfaces are using connection to our IPS centralized Server to perform all management operations.

This GUI being a web based application can be accessed through Web Browser through HTTPS protocol to insure access security. To avoid fraudulence multiple users can not log-in at the same time on a single GUI instance. A synchronization algorithm can be used with locking mechanism to insure mutual exclusion of Server management processes. Each admin user can log-in on the server using GUI to apply its own policy to implement on an IPS client or on Server to manage a significant security event.

This GUI should be having some common global section which reflects the management activities run by other users and IPS clients. Whenever a new attack is detected by Clients and Server applications it should display on this global section. So that other users and clients can synchronize their management activities.

**This Web GUI should give access to following category of Users :**

**Super Admin** – A Super Admin user should be given authority to manage and view all the management activities running by any other user. Two Super Admin users can not login concurrently on IPS Server to avoid fraudulence activities. As the client connects to the Management Server, a prompt for the user name and password is displayed. A Super User account is included by default, but it is possible to set up multiple administrator accounts, each with different roles. There are three main accounts:

**Admin** – having an IPS client administration authority. This role has the ability to administer IPS clients which Admin has been granted access and view the related screenshots.

**Operator** – can view all screens, but may not perform any of IPS management or administration functions.

It is also possible to apply more granular access controls by restricting individual users to specific devices and/or segment groups. Disallowing device access, for example, would prevent a user from seeing and making changes to the device configuration while allowing them to manage and deploy policies. Restricting a user to specific segments or segment groups will ensure that each administrator can only deploy policies to that segment or group of segments (which can span multiple sensors). This means that if a user is restricted to the DMZ segment group he can deploy policies only to the segments which make up that group, making this perfect for large corporate or managed service environments.

### 7.5.2 Tier-2 IPS Centralized Server

The centralized Intrusion Prevention System server will be a Software System implemented on a Server computer. It is made to manage all the Security service policies, Network Attack events, to maintain log information and Protocols. It will be a centralized server in order to service distributed IPS clients all over the network. The IPS administrators can easily manage Centralized management of policies and logs to insure best network security scenario for a large distributed organization.

**The Centralized IPS Server will consist of the following components:**

**1) List Management Module:** This component will manage the Black list, White List and Grey List from the data coming through different client machines which have implemented our system. We are also using the reports published by different organizations providing security solutions to prevent spam. This list can be used by all the instances of our proposed anti spam service, and managed by the administrators.

**2) Web Service Management Module:** We have proposed our anti-spam solution in form of a web service hosted on our web server. This service is having different security criteria and versions for different Web platforms.

Each service will exists so that multiple instances of same service can be easily called from the web applications. We are planning to deploy more services in country/area-wise manner to handle a large network.

**3) Advance Analysis Module:** The System administrators of our service may analyze the different module to further classify the categories of Black,White and Grey lists. The purpose of this module is to update our lists for further analysis and to make trends of Spam attacks.

**4) Response Module:** This module is responsible to provide response to legitimate and illegitimate network traffics. This module is using the Honeypot systems to handle the Spambots.

The entire communication with the other two tiers of the IPS system is encrypted and authenticated to provide an additional level of security. The Centralized Server gathers log records for security events using UDP. Alerts are stored in a MySQL or a commercial database. The data fusion capability allows aggregation and correlation of log data. Consolidation of logs helps to reduce the total number of unique events that the Sensors generate by logically combining large numbers of identical events into a single alert. This summarized data are used for reporting. Security managers can easily analyze these summary reports and, also, drill down to perform detail analysis. The Centralized Server also provides a flexible query manager.

### 7.5.3 Tier-3 IPS Clients

The role of IPS Clients is to monitor the network for network attacks and inform the IPS server. These IPS Clients will be network software components. They can work in both active and passive modes to insure the security in coordination with Centralized IPS Server.

The primary task of IPS Clients is to detect suspicious and anomalous network traffic based on specific rules defined in rule bases of IPS. If the Clients are running in-line, it can also take a predefined action against malicious traffic.

IPS Clients can be deployed as active gateways or passive sniffers. A passive sniffer client connects to a switch or hub in the promiscuous mode and sniffs the network traffic. The Client monitors network traffic, records security events, and can create alarms for attacks. However, because a sniffer client cannot take direct action against the attack, it cannot prevent it. It can only send TCP reset packets through a non-forwarding interface.

In the proposed model, IPS clients will provide unique and global Application_Identification_Number to all the application instances working at the client side. The IPS Clients will make a unique combination of App_id, along with the IP address of the client machine and MAC address of IPS Client machine. This unique combination will be termed as M-key now on in this thesis. The CAPTCHA mechanism is used to identify the spam bots to secure the system. .A Smart CAPTCHA mechanism is used to provide authentication security feature.

**The intelligent M-Key will block the system access in following situations :**

If application failed to give correct CATCHA challenge is 3 attempts. With each fail CAPTCHA challenge, the IPS client will request for tougher category of CAPTCHA challenge.

If IPS client will detect that CAPTCHA challenge is failed and user has restarted the Application to get another global App_Id.

If IPS client will detect that user have changed the IP Address, after the Application Instance is blocked. Such client will be blocked as spammer is believed to gain the Administrator access and able to change the IP address of the client machine. Now this M-Key will differ from older M-Key from which spammer have tried the system access.

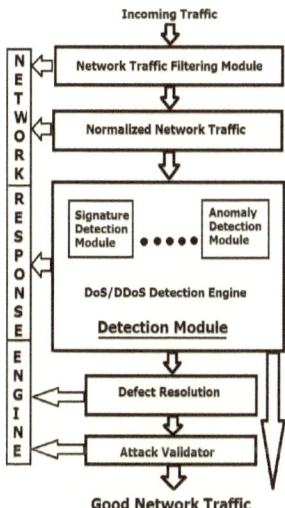

Figure 27 : Working of Proposed IPS

An Intrusion Prevention System help you configure, tune, and manage IPS sensors, Inspection, Prevention, Detection & Security Services Modules, IPS also works as a firewall.

Now a day's malware are being designed to share information among infected nodes, which then attack, infect, and mutate as a group activity. An infected host then starts seeding and starts looking for new victims, or can become one of the many "zombie" nodes that are responsible for most of the spam in this world.

These days' serial attacks are in trend. Just a few malware-hosting sites can infect thousands of hosts and a handful of botnet command-and-control servers can order billions of malicious connections a day. Even if software and attack signature updates are available frequently, an IPS has had

117

to evaluate each attack differently, without knowing if the source of a connection has been infected or not.

**In order to provide a global solution for Network Intrusion Problems it needs a collection of following information:**

To collect these information we need to maintain a SensorBase, which can be a global threat monitoring network. This SensorBase receives constant threat notifications from hundreds of thousands of globally implemented IPS, firewall, web, and email security deployments around the globe, combined with hundreds of partner information feeds, to assemble a comprehensive view of the Internet threat. In turn security analysts convert this contextual data into the threat updates that are sent to every IPS implementation globally.

Traditional Intrusion Prevention Systems do not have enough information to block all attacks with confidence, because they can only block base on their knowledge of behaviors that may be just vague. With proposed solution the IPS Server can provide valuable information about the reputation of the counterparty in every transaction, so that the IPS can block suspicious activity from known attackers.

As the Network Infrastructures become more collaborative, increased risk is expected to increase rapidly. A Globally correlated IPS can detect and manage the day to day evolving threats.

### 7.6  Procedure of Proposed Intrusion Prevention System [104]

**Step 1: Client sends a HttpRequest to IPS**

Whenever an IPS client starts working, it will start an Http Request to the IPS server. With this request IP Address and MAC Address of the IPS client will be sent to the global IPS server.

**Step 2: IPS Server will offer a CAPTCHA challenge**

The Smart CAPTCHA server will generate a CAPTCHA challenge to the IPS Client to ensure that Application is under control of a human and not any spam bot. Total of 3 attempts will be given to the IPS Client to provide correct answer to CAPTCHA challenge.

**Step 3: IPS registers the Application Id of Client App**

The global IPS Server will generate a unique global Application ID for that Client application. No other application communicating with the IPS server can get this identification number i.e. App Id.

**Step 4: If Client enters wrong Captcha, the App_Id is recorded and in response a tougher captcha is generated, sensing a DDoS attack.**

If Client machine enters a wrong captcha the IPS will record the App_Id from which a wrong CAPTCHA response is generated and returns in turn a tougher captcha challenge. Now the DDoS prevention mechanism starts on the Server.

**Step 5: At the maximum 3 try has to be given to the Client Application.**

A Client machine will get maximum of 3 try, one by one with a tougher CAPTCHA challenges.

**Step 6: On failure the App Id, Mac Add and IP Add will be blocked.**

When all the three attempts have been finished and Machine failed to give right CAPTCHA result. The IPS will detect that some SPAM bot is attempting Intrusion Attack. In turn the App_Id, MAC Address and IP Address of machine have been recorded in the Server Database and no further attempt will be provided with the consent of IPS Centralized server.

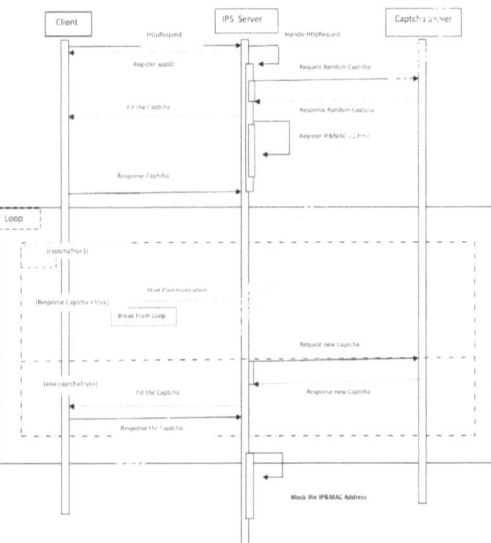

Figure 28: Sequence Diagram of Proposed Intrusion Prevention System[105]

## 7.7 Proposed SPAM Control Solution

As discussed in article 7.1 of this chapter, we are proposing a solution to Control/Minimize the amount of Spam generated online, and therefore accordingly minimizing the DDoS attacks.

After studying the pros and cons of various Spam filtering modules, we have found that most of them are quite effective but Spammers have developed their countermeasures to generate spam.

For the Unsolicited Bulk Emails, Spam databases, Black-White-Grey lists approaches, Content Filtering, Subject Filtering, Email Header analysis, Naïve Bayesian etc techniques are quite effective. But to give more strength to

120

generate Spam historical data, more Spam Sets are required. Also we have to think like a Spammers in order to stop them.

The CAPTCHA is used in most of Web Form to prevent Spammers and Bots to fill the Web forms with junk data and in process to fire junk emails. There are lots of CAPTCHA algorithms to stop the Zombies, Spam-Bots to automatically fill the web forms and generate Spam Emails.

**We have suggested a different approach to stop Spammers; we are going to hit on their Approach of Spamming Behavior. Following are some common behavior of Spammers:**

The spammers are very busy fellows they don't like to sit on a workstation to submit junk data manually.

They have deployed Spam-bots, Zombies, Malware, Adware, etc. to generate Spam Emails.

They like to send Millions of Spam Emails per minute using their malicious softwares.

They keep generating new email-ids on their email servers. Most of their Email-id's have a feature of not accepting the reply, so they mention "Don't-Reply" in subject of Emails.

In most of Spam-Mails the Email header contains different addresses in from and mailed-by fields.

In Most of Spam-mails, the Sender Id contains some popular or attracting female name – Sweety, Love, Kim, Jeniffer, etc.

Figure 29 : Email Headers of Non-Spam-Email

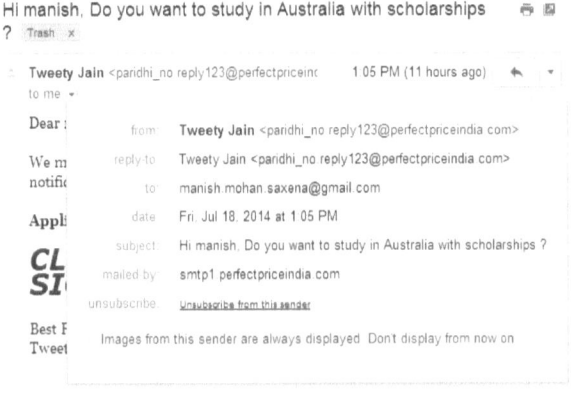

Figure 30 : Email Headers in SPAM Email

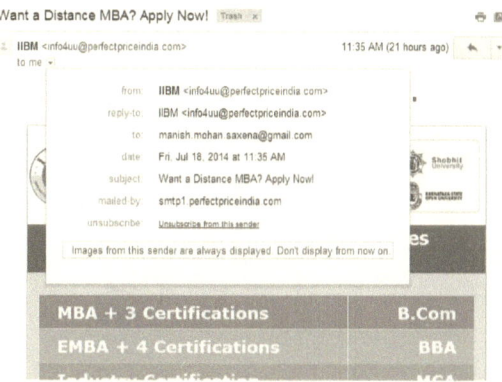

Figure 31 : Email Header for SPAM Mail where Email headers are matching

## 7.8 Architecture of Proposed Spamizer

| Level − 1 | Level − 2 |
|---|---|
| Graphical User Interface based Web Form on User side | Online Spamizer Logic on the Web Server |

Figure 32 : Proposed Spamizer Multi-Level Architecture

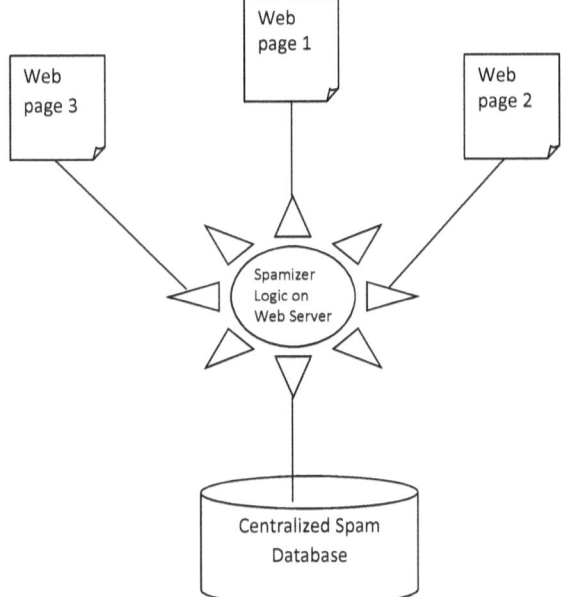

Figure 33 : Proposed Spamizer Block Diagram

## 7.9 Spam Statistics

Let's check the statistical data of Spam generated by Srizbi Spambot:

| | | |
|---|---|---|
| Per day Spam Messages from Srizbi | : | 60 billion |
| | | 60 x 1,000,000,000 messages |
| Per hour Spam Messages from Srizbi | : | 60 x 1,000,000,000 / 24 |
| messages | | 2500000000 messages |
| Per minute Spam Messages from Srizbi | : | 2500000000 / 60 messages |
| | | 41666666.66667 |
| Per Second Spam Messages from Srizbi | : | 694444.44444 |

124

Above statistics shows that only Srizbi tool is generating approximately 7,00,000 messages per second to generate Spam emails.

If an average size of Spam email with some pictures and text is approx 10 kb

Then, Srizbi server needs 7,00,000 x 10 kb  per second bandwidth

Which is, 70,00,000 kbps bandwidth,

Or,  7, 000  Mbps bandwidth

Or, effectively   "7 GBps bandwidth"

Over a Dedicated Leased Line Internet connection with 1 : 1 ratio of Upload and download, with some 10 % fluctuations in bandwidth they need a minimum of 14+1.4 = 15.4 GBps bandwidth connection.

According to BSNL India website, *http://www.bsnl.co.in/opencms/bsnl/BSNL /service /broadband/internet_tariff1.html*

155 Mbps leased line with 1:1 ratio, the charges are Rs. 73,12,500

While we need 100 times more bandwidth,        Rs. 73,12,50,000

Approximately, 73 Lakh Rupees per year.

Now in place of 7,00,000 Spam emails per second, if we can restrict Srizbi server to send only one Spam email per minute per server, and suppose we are having  about 100 target servers, then Spam Emails generated per second comes out to be :

7,00,000 / (60 * 100)                = 116.66667 Spam emails per second

Now the ratio of spam reduction is     = ( 116.66667 * 100 ) / 7,00,000

                                       = 99.98333 %

Which is the actual WoW !!!!!!!

### 7.10 Approach Level 1:  Alternative use of Honeypot

Honeypot is generally used to attract a spammer spam bot, in this dissertation we have proposed a different approach for Honeypot, referred as "HoneyTrap" now on.

Once a spam attack is diagnosed from our Spamizer algorithm, then in spite of showing a warning message to spammer "Access Denied", we will en route this spam attack to a similar application path, a Honeypot, where Spammer's Spambot will feel no difference than the actual application.

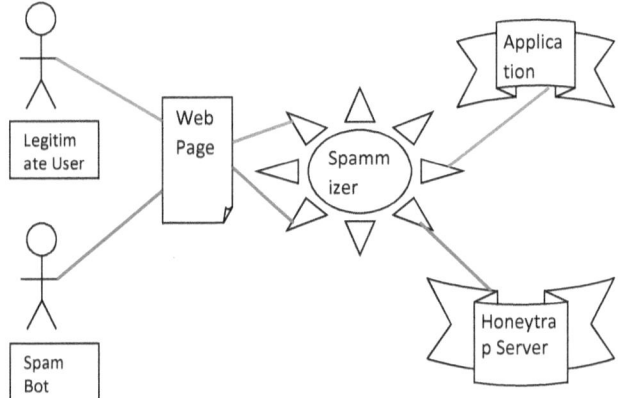

Figure 34 : Alternative use of Honeypot

But the junk contents will not be recorded in the database, and no spam email will generate, still spam bot will receive a message that spammer's "Data is successfully saved". This will not annoy the Spammer and it will keep trying sending spam. This approach will save a considerable amount of spam generated.

A HoneyPot trap or Honeytrap is a technique to detect unauthorized spam attacks by spambots to trick and reveal their identities. As all the legitimate request are sent to main server, the service degradation on Honeypot servers can be regarded due to spam and DDOS attacks by spammers.

We are transferring the Spam Bots to Honey Trap Server when they are trying to come again and again by using same IP Address and MAC Address which we have maintained in our IP Blacklist or MAC Blacklist.

### 7.11 Approach Level 2: Easy Spam Prevention Using Hidden Form Fields

"A Spambot cannot distinguish the difference between whether or not form fields are optional or required, so spambot just fills all of them. If you think about it, every website is different when it comes to marking required fields; some do it with asterisks, some with red text, some with the still poorly supported HTML5 attribute "required", and others don't bother to mark them at all, but rather redirect you back if you happen to miss one. It only makes sense that a bot would get tripped up on such a thing and simply not even try.

Not only do spambots struggle with recognizing required fields, but they also struggle with reading CSS or JavaScript, at least for now. The simplest solution, then, is to add a completely arbitrary field to each form and then to hide it using any number of such methods, for example:

<input type = "text" name= "haha" style = "display:none;">

Alternatively, you could opt for something a little more complex like giving the field an ID or a class which would then force the bot to scan through your CSS files to determine the element's visibility.

You could also use Javascript to remove the arbitrary field from display as the page loads, for example:

```
<div id="hahaDiv">
<label for="haha">Please Leave this field blank</label>
<input type="text" name="haha" id="haha">
</div>
<script>
(function () {
var e = document.getElementById("hahaDiv");
e.parent Node.removeChild(e);
})();
</script>
```

Notice how the field in the example has been given a label instructing the user to leave the field blank on the off chance they have JavaScript disabled.

Now you can rest assured that if the field ever has a value when the form submission reaches your server then the transaction can be discarded as junk. No matter which method you use the bot now has the added task of figuring out whether or not a given field is visible and/or required, which you could argue would take some pretty advanced AI or a more targeted approach on behalf of the spammer.

It might also help to randomize where the arbitrary field is displayed and how it is named so that it is even less predictable.

Of course, no solution is completely foolproof, as spam is sometimes still manually submitted by humans, so it never hurts to have more than one prevention procedure in place. To add another layer of protection, when spam is detected you should still go ahead and redirect the bot as though it were a successful form submission; I don't like to give them any reason to probe." [106]

### 7.12 Approach Level 3: Using Difference in Initial & Final MAC Addresses

Generally programmers are checking the IP addresses to prevent Spam, but We have tried to compare the MAC addresses.

❖ Record the MAC Address at the Initial Time
❖ Process the Form
❖ Record the MAC Address at the Final Time

If the MAC Addresses are different, then user is a Spambot, as MAC address depends on the Network Interface Card, and MAC address is embedded on the manufacturing time. This is not possible to change within the processing of a Contact Form. It must be a Spamming bot uses Cloud structure and it keep changing the MAC address with shell scripts.

128

### 7.13 Approach Level 4: Using Application Time Difference's

It's a new approach for Spam Detection,

Here we are recording the 1st Time Stamp when user starts working on a Form

Then we are recording the final Time Stamp when user submits a Form

Application Time = Submit Time – Initial Time

There is an Average Time of every URL containing a Contact Form, stored in a table by the admin. So we can access it through a SQL query.

If ( Application Time < = (90/100) * Average Time )

Then, It is an entry which can be done only using a Spam Bot, so HoneyTrap module will handle it. Update the Black List of IP Address & MAC Address.

Else, It is a legitimate entry and it can be stored in Database.

### 7.14 Spamizer Algorithm : Web Spam Control

**Step 1:** User generates HTTP Request for a Web Form through hyperlink for a page

URL (e.g. www.manishsaxena.in/webform/contact.php)

**Step 2:** Web Server containing the URL receives a HTTP Request

**Step 3:** Web Server Collects the Initial Time Tini from Server Clock at the time of HTTP Request, when web form got focus.

**Step 4:** Web Server creates a unique Form_ID for same URL

**Step 5:** Web Server collects MACinitial and IPinitial from User end, store IPinitial in list of current day.

**Step 6:** If IPinitial is present more than 03 times on in list of same day, inform User that Maximum number of attempts to contact reached, reject the HTTP request.

**Step 7:** Check If MACinitial and IPinitial exists in Black list.

**Step 8:** If MACinitial and IPinitial present in the list, Honeytrap Module activated.

Go To Step 29

Else Application_Id generated(MACinitial Add + IPinitial Add + Form_ID)

**Step 9:** Web Form code transferred from Web Server to User end.

Process Fork Started.

| Section A | Section B |
|---|---|
| **Step 10a:** User enters the form data at User<br>  end.<br>**Step 11a:** Form field validation ensures<br> correct and mandatory data to be entered by user.<br>**Step 12a:** User faces the CAPTCHA challenge.<br>**Step 13a:** If CAPTCHA challenge fails, increase CAPTCHA counter by 1<br>**Step 14a:** If CAPTCHA challenge counter<br><= 3 , GOTO Step 12a<br>**Step 15a:** Else Block IP Add for 01 hours.<br>End the Session.<br>Update IP Grey List<br>GoTo Step 29<br>**Step 16a:** Else User POST the form to Web Server.<br>**Step 17a:** If hidden field is having some data,it's a spam bot who filled the data<br> Then, HoneyTrap Module Activated.<br> End If.<br>**Step 18a:** Web Server records the submit time $T_{sub}$ at the time of POST. It calculates the Application time | **Step 10b:** Search URL in URL Database<br>**Step 11b:** If available fetch Avg Time for the URL<br><br><br>**Step 12b:** Else Inform Admin about new URL && Assume Avg Time =2 |

130

| $( T_{app} = T_{sub} - T_{ini} )$ | |
|---|---|

Process Join Done

**Step 19:** From Section A we are getting Application time from a user, and from parallel executing Section B we are getting Average time of a form from historical data stored by admin in training mode.

Now Compare if,

Application Time $< = (0.9 \times$ Average Time)

**Step 20:** Then, Spam Table updated & Honey Trap Module Activated.

GoTo Step 29

**Step 21:** Else, check

If, Application time $> = $ TTL , (Time To Last for the URL)

**Step 22:** Then, Increase Attempt Counter by 1

**Step 23:** Compare If No of attempts $< = 3$

**Step 24:** Then, Reset the Web Form, GoTo Step 1

**Step 25:** Else, Block MAC Add & IP Add for 24 hours,

Update IP Grey List & MAC Grey List

**Step 26:** GoTo Step 29

**Step 27:** Else, Submit Information in the Database

**Step 28:** Delete Incomplete entries in Previous Attempts

**Step 29:** Stop the Algorithm

**7.15 Use Case Diagrams**

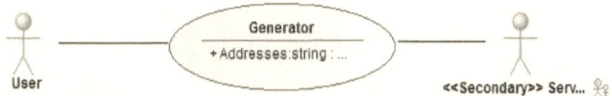

The above use case depicts the interaction of client (termed as user )to the server .client generate HTTP request to the server  that collect initial IP and MAC addresses from clients .

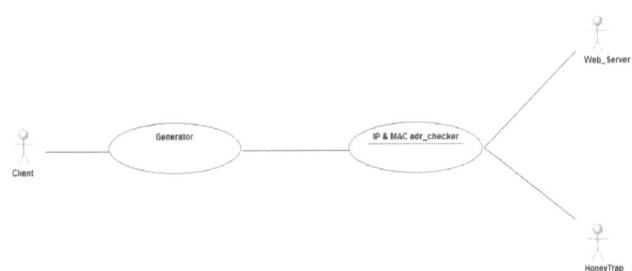

It describe the generation of IP & MAC address process and also check if it is blocked then HoneyTrap module activated with interconnection of web server.

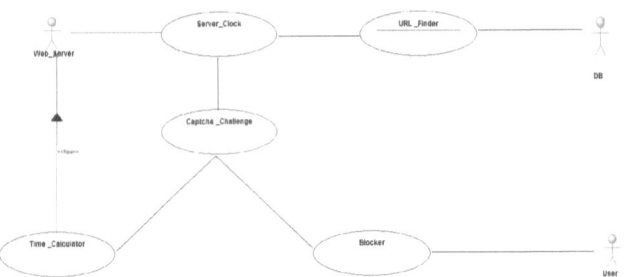

There are three actor in usecase namely User, DB and WebServer. Web server has a clock to compute the time in Captcha submission and verified it by the URL Finder and store it into the Database. if any error found then block & message to user.

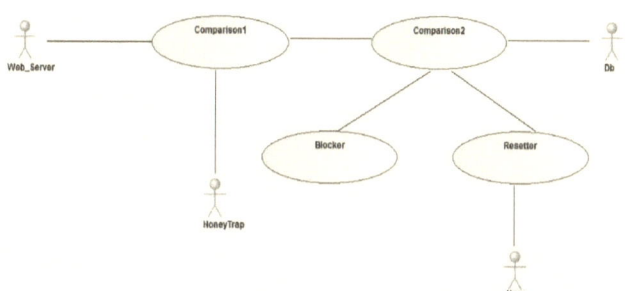

This use case has a WebServer which compare the Application time to the Avg.time   If App.time<=Avg. time then update the Spam table and activated the HoneyTrap Module,

If not then compare App. time with TTL .If App.time >=TTL then increase the counter and check attempts <=3;Block Mac and IP Adddress for 24 Hours otherwise submit information in the Database.

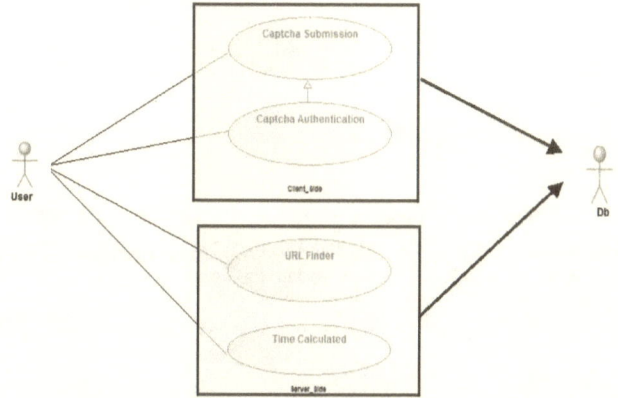

133

There are two parallel operation perform with the help of Fork. One is Captcha Module and another is URL Finder and both information goes into the Database.

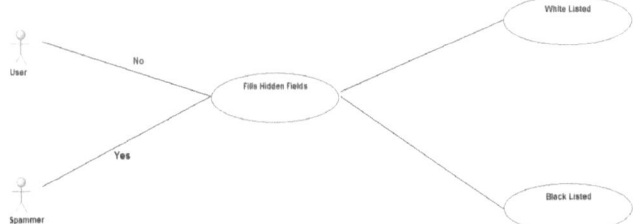

There is another technique Fills Hidden Fields it check & store into the Whitelist &Blacklist according to User and Spammer.

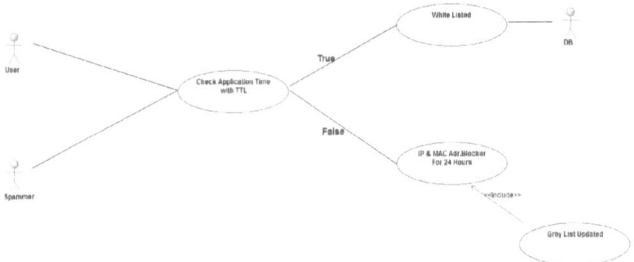

If there is no value in Hidden Fields check App.time with TTL .ifApp.time >=TTL then store into Whitelist and submit to Database, otherwise Block IP & MAC Adr. For 24 Hours & update the Grey List.

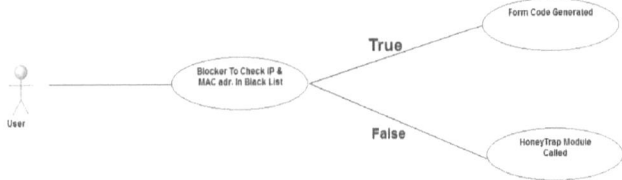

There is a User's IP & MAC Adr.,if it found in Blacklist then HoneyTrap Module Activated otherwise Generate the Form Code.

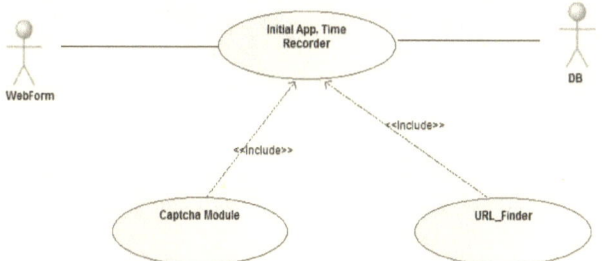

There is a Captcha Module and another is URL Finder and both included with Initial App.time Recorder which interact with WebForm and submit into the Database.

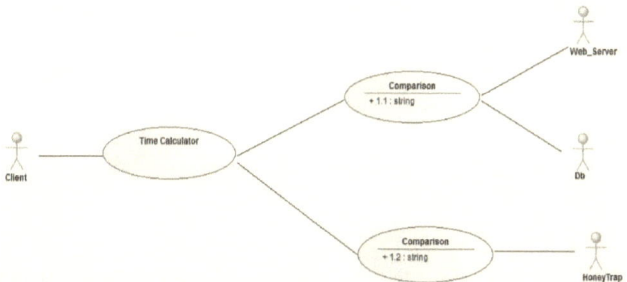

There is a Time Calculator which compare the time according to the Client 's Initial time and Submit time, one goes to Database and other activated the HoneyTrap Module .

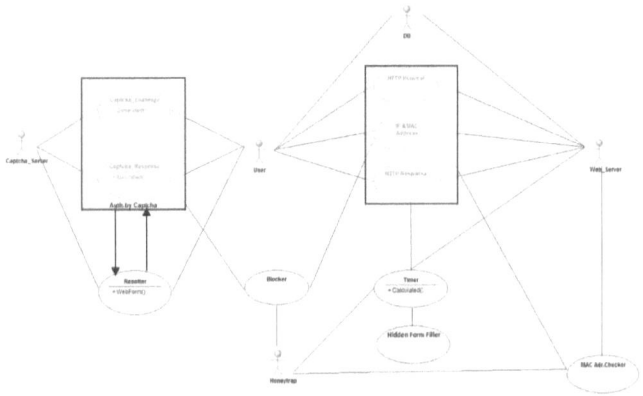

Overall Mechanism of Web Page Process

⟨?⟩

**UML Diagram :** 2. Activity Diagram for Web Page Submission

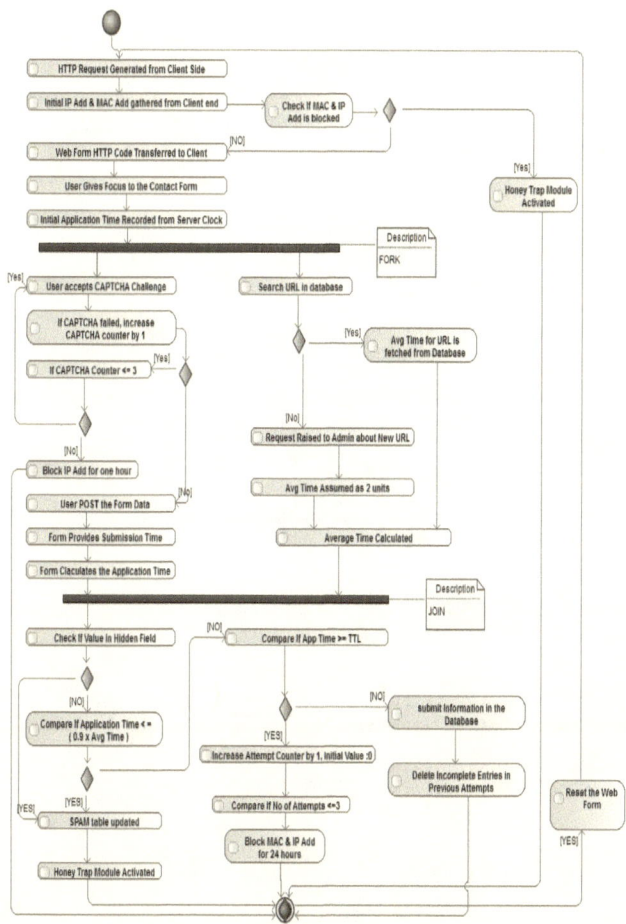

Figure 35 Activity diagram for Web Page Registration
137

**UML Diagram :** 3. Sequence Diagram for Web Page Submission

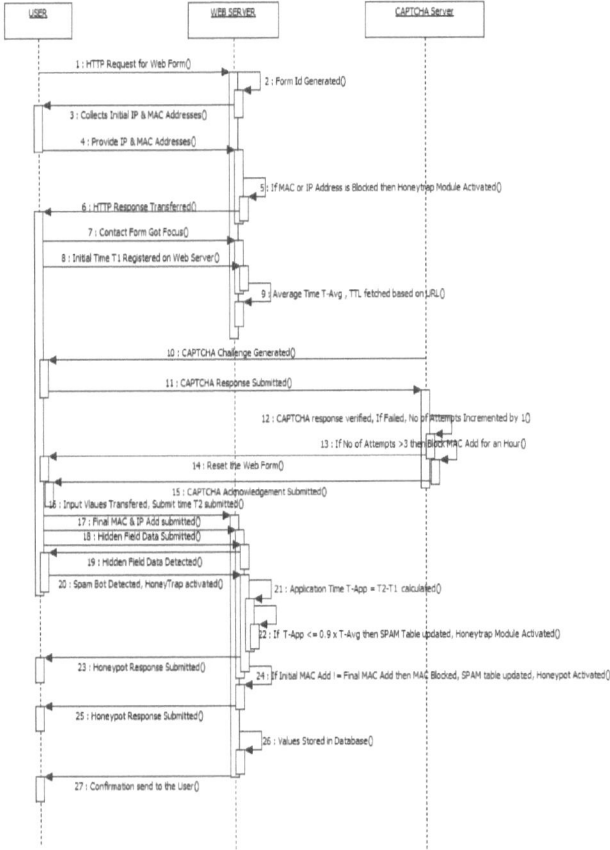

Figure 36 : Sequence Diagram for Web Page Registration

### 7.16 Best Practices for a Spamizer:

❖ Understanding of terms used for signature status
❖ Dealing with memory allocation errors when compiling signatures
❖ Total number of signatures can be compiled
❖ Dealing with signature failing to compile
❖ Configuration steps
❖ Dealing with IOS IPS policy applied at the wrong direction and/or interface
❖ Dealing with signature that do not fire with matching traffic
❖ Dealing with Packet/Connections dropped due to packets arriving out of order

### 7.17 Data Dictionary

Table to Store URL Data : url_tbl

| Field | Field Type |
|---|---|
| Id | bigint(20) |
| url | varchar(255) |
| avg_time | int(11) |
| ttl_time | int(11) |
| created_date | Datetime |

Table to Store Non-Spam (White) Data : white_data

| Field | Type |
|---|---|
| id | bigint(20) |
| ip_ini | varchar(25) |
| ip_fin | varchar(25) |
| mac_ini | varchar(25) |
| mac_fin | varchar(25) |

139

| | | |
|---|---|---|
| | url | varchar(255) |
| | name | varchar(100) |
| | email | varchar(150) |
| | mobile | varchar(10) |
| | message | Text |
| | created_date | datetime |

Table to Store Spam Data : spam_data

| | Field | Type |
|---|---|---|
| | id | bigint(20) |
| | ip_ini | varchar(25) |
| | ip_fin | varchar(25) |
| | mac_ini | varchar(25) |
| | mac_fin | varchar(25) |
| | url | varchar(255) |
| | name | varchar(100) |
| | email | varchar(150) |
| | mobile | varchar(10) |
| | message | Text |
| | created_date | datetime |

Table to Store Spam Data : spam_data

| | Field | Type |
|---|---|---|
| | id | bigint(20) |
| | ip_ini | varchar(25) |

| | | |
|---|---|---|
| | ip_fin | varchar(25) |
| | mac_ini | varchar(25) |
| | mac_fin | varchar(25) |
| | url | varchar(255) |
| | name | varchar(100) |
| | email | varchar(150) |
| | mobile | varchar(10) |
| | message | Text |
| | created_date | datetime |

Table to IP Blacklist : ipbl

| | Field | Type |
|---|---|---|
| | id | bigint(20) |
| | ip_ini | varchar(25) |
| | ip_fin | varchar(25) |
| | mac_ini | varchar(25) |
| | mac_fin | varchar(25) |
| | url | varchar(255) |
| | name | varchar(100) |
| | email | varchar(150) |
| | mobile | varchar(10) |
| | message | Text |
| | created_date | datetime |

Table to IP Blacklist : ipbl

|  | Field | Type |
|---|---|---|
|  | id | bigint(20) |
|  | ip_ini | varchar(25) |
|  | me ip_date | date |
|  | ip_time | time |

Table to MAC Blacklist : macbl

|  | Field | Type |
|---|---|---|
|  | id | bigint(20) |
|  | mac_add | varchar(25) |
|  | mac_date | date |
|  | mac_time | time |

Table to IP Greylist : ipgl

|  | Field | Type |
|---|---|---|
|  | id | bigint(20) |
|  | ip_add | varchar(25) |
|  | ip_date | date |
|  | ip_time | time |
|  | Ip_gl_time | Int |

### 7.18  Application Area where this Approach is recommended:

### 7.18.1 Preventing Spam Emails :

To increase the search engine rank of websites, Spammers are sending bulk emails to people to get some web traffic, which is done using Spam bots for UBE. This can be controlled by using the proposed technique. Now the display of Contact Emails can be avoided on the webpage and developer can provide a spam controlling Web contact form as suggested. Applying CAPTCHA, Filtering IP Addresses and Hidden Form Field are the present solutions, but using a complete Spamizer algorithm can control Email Spam is a better way.

### 7.18.2  Protecting Web Registrations

The websites who are providing free newsletters, or any other free online services just by registering a new email address in a text box on their websites, suffered most from this problem, the popular solution is email verification, where sender gets a link on their email id and after clicking a link their email id gets verified, but what about a server sending 1 Million Email Verifications in a day, or in a minute as Spammers can sending more than that within a Second. Such spam attack can degrade the Web Server performance, so the proposed solution is a better solution even in this case.

### 7.18.3  E-ticketing

One of the most popular website in India, www.irctc.co.in, which is one of the most used e-commerce website in India, is providing E-ticketing for Indian Railways. In the prime time, 08:00 AM to 10 AM and 19:00PM to 20:00 PM, i.e. the starting and closing time of reservations, they get maximum traffic, spammers are using DDoS attacks to populate their reservation server with a bombardment of Spam Searching, Spam E-Mails etc just to degrade the performance of their website. So that people can't get their reservation on time, and their reservation agents can earn from those users. The proposed anti-spam solution can help in this situation.

### 7.18.4  Online Polls

With an auto-form filler spam bot, a spammer can fill the desired option out of given options on any online poll. This will break the purpose of

Online Polling and their preferred option will get the maximum votes. The proposed solution can solve such polling attacks.

### 7.18.5 Dictionary Attacks

In case of password systems, spammers are using the dictionary attacks by providing all possible dictionary words one by one just to break the password and to get the access in any online application. The proposed solution can solve this problem as well.

There are many other online scenarios where the proposed solution can work.

## 7.19 Comparison of different IDS/IPS Technologies with M-Key Solution

| Design Parameters | Snort Inline (IDS) | Packet Alarm (IDS) | Hawk Eye Solutions (IDS) | Strata Guard (IPS) | Proposed M-Key Soln (IDS/IPS) |
|---|---|---|---|---|---|
| Anomalies Detection | √ | √ | √ | | √ |
| Firewall Support | | | | | √ |
| Protection Against DoS Attack | | √ | √ | | √ |
| Protection Against DDoS Attack | | | | | √ |
| Personalized Rule Creation | √ | | √ | | √ |
| Vulnerabilities Scanner | | √ | √ | | √ |
| Multi Sensor Management | | √ | | | √ |
| Remote Management | | √ | | | √ |
| Report Generation | | | √ | | √ |
| Inline IPS Mode | | | | | √ |
| Passive IDS Mode | √ | √ | √ | | √ |
| Custom Rules | √ | | | | √ |
| Automated Tuning | | | | | √ |
| Secure Authentication Service | | | | | √ |
| CAPTCHA Support | | | | | √ |
| Expert System Capabilities | | | | | √ |

# SCREEN SHOTS OF RESEARCH WORK

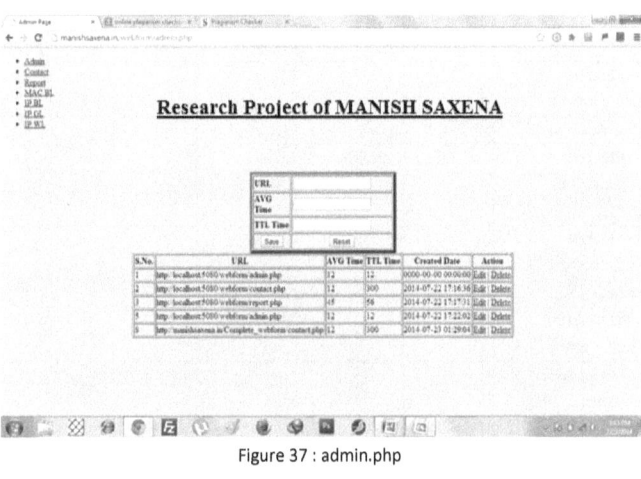

Figure 37 : admin.php

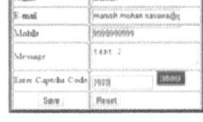

Figure 38: Inserting data in contact.php

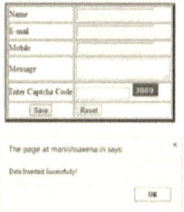

Figure 39: Confirmation of Data Inserted in contact.php

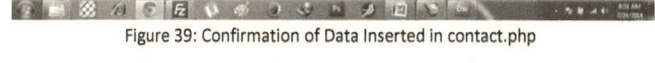

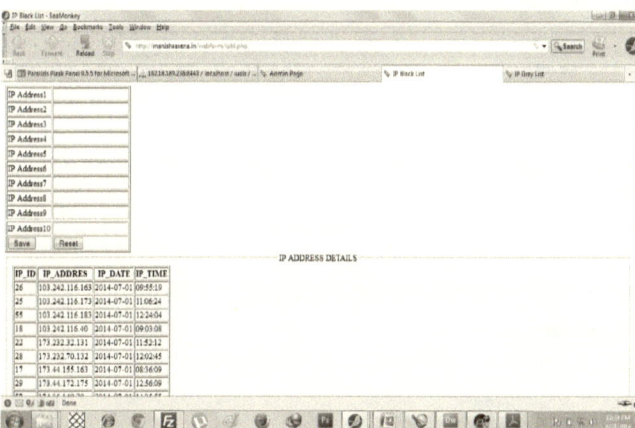

Figure 40: IP Black List Snapshot

# CHAPTER – 08
# RESULTS

In the previous chapter we have discussed different approaches to handle the Spam emails sent through Spam Bots. Though the real challenge will come once the application will run on such a server where millions of hits are coming per second. Still, with a combination of all four approaches discussed earlier, none of Spam Email have been generated so far. Only human can do spam if the logic of anti-spamming is open to them.

More than 30,000 impressions of Spam IP addresses and Spam Email addresses have been gathered by the application so far.

The proposed system has also cleared all the Testing Criteria's. The test reports are shown in this chapter.

The whole system is made using UML diagrams, so its always possible to change the design for a better security level. All the diagrams have been made using Modelio 3.1 version, an open source UML design software which verifies the syntax error free diagrams.

The proposed solution is implemented as an application and presently hosted on

www.manishsaxena.in/webform/contact.php

**On the basis of given formula, following are the observed values:**
If [Application_Time] < =
[(Min. Application_Time * Reduction Percentage)]
then, "Spam Attempt"

**Observed Data:**

This data is recorded by requesting online users with different typing speed, with different operating environments, and some of users were requested to use Browser Cache, some users were requested to use RoboForm type auto form filler applicant ions. Some spammers have also attempted filling the data, on continuous failure they have hacked the server once.

The project is hosted online on my website

*www.manishsaxena.in/webform/contact.php*

| S. No | No. of Attempts | Reduction Factor as Percentage | No of Spam Emails | False Positive |
|-------|-----------------|-------------------------------|-------------------|----------------|
| 1. | 1000 | 90 % | 06 | 04 |
| 2. | 1000 | 80 % | 02 | NIL |
| 3. | 1000 | 50% | NIL | NIL |
| 4. | 1000 | 4 Seconds | NIL | NIL |

TABLE – 01 : OBSERVED SPAM STATISTICS

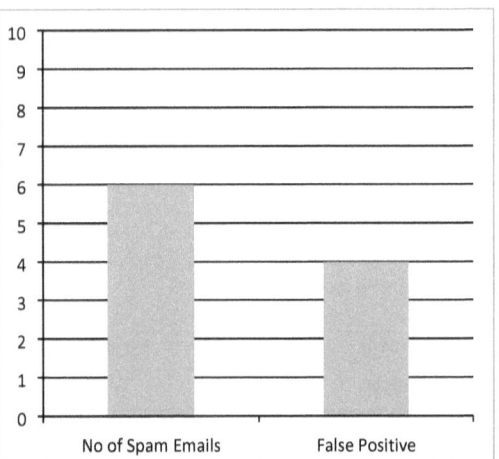

Figure 41 : Observed SPAM Statistics with 90% Reduction Factor

**Findings :**

If we have given 90 % relaxation in Minimum Application Time during 1000 online attempts, 06 spam messages recorded, out of which 04 messages were false positive.

This was recorded because user have opted auto-fill property in their browsers.☒

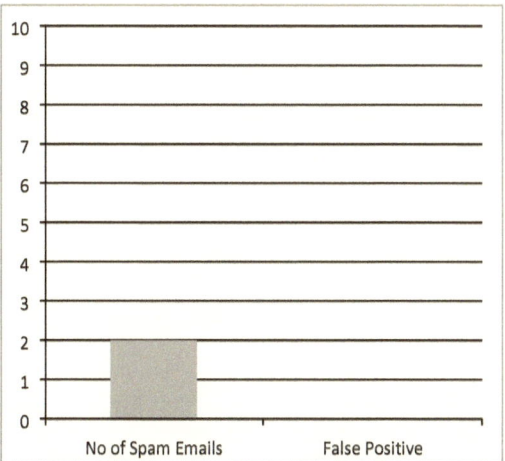

Figure 42 : Observed SPAM Statistics with 80% Reduction Factor

**Findings :**

If we have given 80 % relaxation in Minimum Application Time during 1000 online attempts, 02 spam messages were recorded, out of which None was false positive, which was recorded.

Which was recorded because user have opted for auto-form filler application such as RoboForm9.

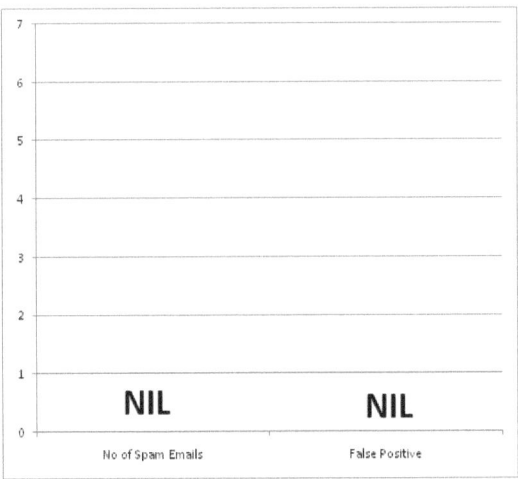

Figure 43 : Observed SPAM Statistics with 50% Reduction Factor

**Findings :**

If we have given 50 % relaxation in Min. Application Time during 1000 online attempts, NONE spam messages was recorded.

May be even after auto-form filler application user has to take a CAPTCHA challenge.

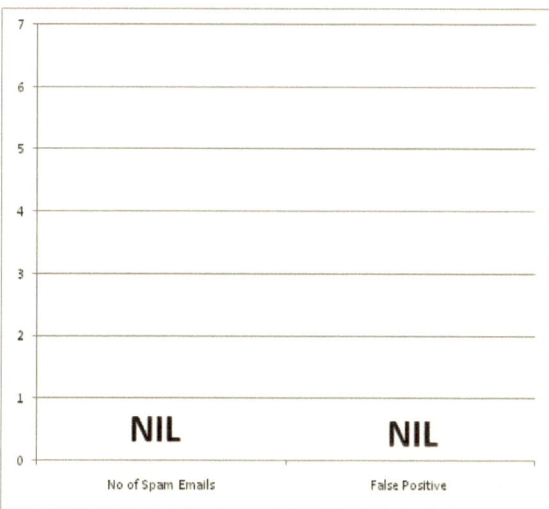

Figure 44 : Observed SPAM Statistics with specific 4 Seconds

**Findings :**

If we have taken 04 seconds as Min. Application Time again NONE spam messages was recorded.

Now only some real spam bot application can submit a form within this much time. Even they have to deploy human by some trick to accept the CAPTCHA challenge.

**Key Findings :**

The key findings of this experiment are as follows:

During application training we have observed that no human can fill up a form in less than Min. Application Time.

If we have given 90 % relaxation in Min. Application Time during 1000 online attempts, 06 spam messages recorded, out of which 04 messages were

153

false positive, which was recorded because user have opted auto-fill property in their browsers.

If we have given 80 % relaxation in Min. Application Time during 1000 online attempts, 02 spam messages were recorded, out of which None was false positive, which was recorded. Here user have opted auto-form filler application such as RoboForm9.

If we have given 50 % relaxation in Min. Application Time during 1000 online attempts, NONE spam messages was recorded. May be even after auto-form filler application user has to take a CAPTCHA challenge.

If we have taken 04 seconds as Min. Application Time again NONE spam messages was recorded. Now only some real spam bot application can submit a form within this much time. Even they have to deploy human by some trick to accept the CAPTCHA challenge.

These results support the hypothesis that CAPTCHA is not the ultimate solution of user authentication, as it can be easily compromised by online users of CAPTCHA solving companies. So we need a solution for such companies.

## 8.1 Software Testing Results

In Software testing we evaluate software to detect if there is some difference between the given input and expected output by assessing the feature of some software item. Testing also assess the quality of the product. Software testing is a part of software development life cycle. We can also say that software testing is a verification and validation process.

### 8.1.1 Verification

In Verification process we make sure that the product satisfies the conditions mentioned in the start of the development phase or to make sure that the product is behaving the way we want.

### 8.1.2 Validation

In Validation process we make sure that the product satisfies the requirements at the end of the development phase or to make sure that the product is built as per given customer requirements.

### 8.1.3 Basics of software testing

There can be two basics of software testing: Blackbox testing and Whitebox testing.

### Blackbox Testing

Black box testing is a testing technique that ignores the coding or source code or internal mechanism of the testing system and focuses on the output generated against any input just by executing the system. Blackbox Testing is also known as functional testing

### Whitebox Testing

In White box testing we take care of the source code and internal functionality of a system. It is also known as Glassbox Testing or structural testing.

Black box testing is generally used for validation purpose and white box testing is generally used for verification purpose.

### 8.1.4 Web Functional Testing

Web Functional testing is a process to test Web applications to detect if your web application is functionally correct. Web Functional testing involves carrying set of tasks and comparing the result of same with the expected output and ability to repeat same set of tasks multiple times with different data input and same level of accuracy. Implementing functional testing for your application early in the software development cycle speeds up development, improves quality and reduces risks towards the end of the cycle.

Web Functional Testing can be performed both manually with a human tester or could be performed automatically with use of a software program.

### 8.1.5 Following types of validations are used in Functional Testing:

**Page validation :** In case of Page Validation you can validate size of the page, count of elements on the page, links , images, input elements, forms etc. can be validated.

**On the contact.php page:**

| | |
|---|---|
| No of Images: | None |
| No of Links: | None |
| No of Forms: | 01 |
| No of Elements: | 05 |
| No of Input Elements: | 06 |
| Size of Web Page : | 6.56 KB |

**On the honey_pot.php page:**

| | |
|---|---|
| No of Images: | None |
| No of Links: | None |
| No of Forms: | 01 |
| No of Elements: | 05 |
| No of Input Elements: | 06 |
| Size of Web Page : | 3.51 KB |

**Text validation :** To find if a particular text or value is present on the page or not you can use this validation

| | |
|---|---|
| Heading Text: | Present |
| Label Text: | All Present |
| Button Text: | All Present |

**Attribute validation :** This type of validation is useful in case you need to validate properties like innerText or value etc. of specific HTML element in page

Name Text Box: Mandatory, User Have filled only characters, no special characters, no numeric values have been given

Email Text Box: Email Address have been given in proper format.

Email is verified by sending an email to user.

Mobile Text Box : Proper 10 Digit Mobile Number has been given. Number is not starting with 0

Submit Button: Data is submitting by presseing Submit Button

Reset Button: Data is resetting by pressing Reset Button.

**Date validation :** Using this kind of validation you can compare the date value present on page against today's date in different formats.

Date Validation: Proper Date Format is used. DD/MM/YYYY

Time Validation: Proper Time Format is used. HH:MM

Database Query validation : Here you can validate if the result set returned as a result of query execution is valid or not.

**Insert query:** Insert Query is working in contact.php, checked the values in the Database.

Insert Query is working in admin.php, checked the values in the Database.

Insert Query is working in macbl.php, checked the values in the Database.

Insert Query is working in ipbl.php, checked the values in the Database.

Insert Query is working in ipgl.php, checked the values in the Database.

Insert Query is working in ipwl.php, checked the values in the Database.

Insert Query is NOT working in honeytrap.php, checked the values in the Database.

**Select Query:**

Select Query is working in admin.php, checked the values in the Database.

Select Query is working in contact.php, checked the values in the Database.

Select Query is working in honeytrap.php, checked the values in the Database.

Select Query is working in macbl.php, checked the values in the Database.

Select Query is working in ipbl.php, checked the values in the Database.

Select Query is working in ipgl.php, checked the values in the Database.

Select Query is working in ipwl.php, checked the values in the Database.

Functional Web Testing Ok

**8.1.6 System Testing :** Cross Browser Testing

Application is made in PHP as Front End

And My SQL as Back End.

**It's working on these Operating Systems:**

MS Windows 8.0/ 7.0/ Vista/ XP SP3/

Red Hat Linux 6.0

**Its working on these browsers:**

Internet Explorer 8.0

Mozilla Firefox 28.0

Google Chrome 36.0

Sea Monkey 2.25

System Testing Done

**8.1.7 Stress Testing**

Stress testing is the testing to evaluate how system behaves under unfavorable conditions. Testing is conducted at beyond limits of the specifications. It falls under the class of black box testing.

Stress Testing Done

**8.1.8 Performance Testing**

Performance testing is the testing to assess the speed and effectiveness of the system and to make sure it is generating results within a specified time as in performance requirements. It falls under the class of black box testing.

Performance Testing Ok.

### 8.1.9 Usability Testing

Usability testing is performed to the perspective of the client, to evaluate how the GUI is user-friendly? How easily can the client learn? After learning how to use, how proficiently can the client perform? How pleasing is it to use its design? This falls under the class of black box testing.

User JoinIndia Technological Solutions, Mumbai is satisfied with its User Interface.

### 8.1.10 Acceptance Testing

Acceptance testing is often done by the customer to ensure that the delivered product meets the requirements and works as the customer expected. It falls under the class of black box testing.

User JoinIndia Technological Solutions, Mumbai is satisfied with its Working.

### 8.1.11  Regression Testing

Regression testing is the testing after modification of a system, component, or a group of related units to ensure that the modification is working correctly and is not damaging or imposing other modules to produce unexpected results. It falls under the class of black box testing.

Regression Testing Done

### 8.1.12  Beta Testing

Beta testing is the testing which is done by end users, a team outside development, or publicly releasing full pre-version of the product which is known as beta version. The aim of beta testing is to cover unexpected errors. It falls under the class of black box testing.

Beta Testing Done.

## 8.2 Cyclomatic Complexity of Web Form Activity Diagram

In an Activity diagrams with forks & joins,

Activities = vertices     ;         Forks = vertices ;

Joins = vertices          ;         flows = edges.

Connected components are all the components at which control starts and stops. (Usually 2 for an activity diagram with 1 Start node and 1 End node.)

"The Cyclomatic number V (G) of a graph G with n vertices, e edges and p connected components is

$$V(G) = e - n + p."$$

Therefore ...

V(G)     = flows - vertices +  connected components.

$$= 49 - 41 + 2$$

$$= 10$$

As per McCabe [107], programmers should count the complexity of the modules they are developing, and split them into smaller modules whenever the cyclomatic complexity of the module exceeded 10

Therefore we don't need to break the algorithm into sub parts.

Database iudb

Table structure for table url_tbl

| Field | Type | Null | Default |
|---|---|---|---|
| id | bigint(20) | Yes | NULL |
| url | varchar(255) | Yes | NULL |
| avg_time | int(11) | Yes | NULL |
| ttl_time | int(11) | Yes | NULL |
| created_date | datetime | Yes | NULL |

Database Backup iudb

Table structure for table ipbl

| Field | Type | Null | Default |
|---|---|---|---|
| id | bigint(2) | Yes | NULL |
| ip_add | varchar(25) | Yes | NULL |
| ip_date | date | Yes | NULL |
| ip_time | time | Yes | NULL |

Database iudb

Table structure for table ip_gl

| Field | Type | Null | Default |
|---|---|---|---|
| id | bigint(20) | Yes | NULL |
| ip_add | varchar(25) | Yes | NULL |
| ip_date | date | Yes | NULL |
| ip_time | time | Yes | NULL |
| Block_time | int(6) | Yes | NULL |

# CHAPTER – 9
# CONCLUSION & FUTURE SCOPE

In the recent world with talented Bad Boys and Good Guys, the Internet is developed as the major communication source. Beyond communication, Internet surfing has become a life style of many – working most of time on social websites, blogs, and newsgroups as all. Everyone likes to be updated with almost everything happening in their surroundings. The increased used of Smartphones and Tablets have made people always connected to the Internet.

There comes the risk, as people are sharing everything on internet, they like to store all personal and private information's on internet itself, there comes the role of Bad Boys, they like to access such information, like to alter them; sometimes for their profits, sometimes for 'aiwain' aka for no reason. Through Spamming Bad Boys are doing DDOS attacks on servers, on websites, to interrupt them, to get their access.

Though we have tested our research idea online, but once it will be implemented on the real production web server on some high search ranking website, it will face an encounter by major Spam bots. On the basis of Application Time criteria, spam bots will try to compromise the anti-spam security standards, still if we will restrict them sending 7L spam messages to 350 spam messages per second as proposed, it will still be a success. We are planning to add more security levels to this solution in coming time. We are in process to make a new CAPTCHA which will further reduce the spam message generation, which can easily compromise the treats of CAPTCHA solving companies. We are also planning for a Browser Plug-in to easily access the MAC Addresses from client end to add more security.

Denial of service attacks are a huge threat to the internet as a whole. In order to thwart these attacks over all internet security must be promoted and potential targets must be prepared for the potential attacks. It is critical that security methods evolve with the evolving denial of service attacks to be truly secure. Formal Classification by some Community related organization is necessary in the field of Distributed Denial of Service which is proposed in our research work [108], [109], [110], [111], [112], [113].

We have proposed a solution for Web Spamming where a Spammer is using Spam Bots to send spam emails through the contact form / feedback forms given on websites, CMS solutions like Wordpress and Joomla, News Groups, Blogs, etc. We are sure that this solution will solve the problem of Spamming up to a great extent. As we have worked on a Behavioural approach of a spammer, just to stop sending him bulk emails at once.

There are scopes of future development as well, We are planning to make a Web Service which makes the webpage lighter to work, and will provide extra security by implementing Object Oriented Approaches.

Annexure – I : Spamizer : An approach to handle web form spam
Proceedings of the 9th INDIACom; INDIACom-2015
2015 2nd International Conference on "Computing for Sustainable Global
Development", 11$^{th}$ – 13$^{th}$ March, 2015

# SPAMIZER : AN APPROACH TO HANDLE WEB FORM SPAM

|                                      |                                    |
|--------------------------------------|------------------------------------|
| **Manish Saxena**                    | **P. M. Khan**                     |
| MCA Department, FGIET                 | Computer Center, A.M.U.            |
| Raebareli, India                     | Aligarh, India                     |
| Email Id: gmail@manishsaxena.in      | Email Id: pmkhan.cc@amu.ac.in      |

**Abstract** – The Spam Emails are regularly causing huge losses to business on a regular basis. The Spam filtering is an automated technique to identity SPAM and HAM (Non-Spam). The Web Spam filters can be categorized as: Content based spam filters and List based spam filters. In this research work, we have studied the spam statistics of a famous Spambot 'Srizbi'. We have also discussed different approaches for Spam Filtering and finally proposed a new algorithm which is made on the basis of behavioral approaches of Spammers and to restrict the budding economical growth of Spam generating company's. We have used the hidden Honeypot and a Honeytrap module to minimize the spam generated from Contact and Feedback forms on public and social networking CMS websites.

**Keywords** – Spamizer, Spam bots, Honeypots, HoneyTrap, Web Form Comment Spam, Srizbi.

## NOMENCLATURE

UBE – Unsolicited Bulk Email

SPAM – Unsolicited, Unwanted Email

HAM – Non spam Message

CAPTCHA – Completeely Automated Public Turing test to tell Computers and Human Apart

## I. INTRODUCTION

In the electronic communications medium Spamming is sending unsolicited and usually unwanted messages or emails in bulk without taking consent of the recipients sometimes referred as UBE or Unsolicited Bulk Emails. One of the most common spam is sending a Spam Email. The objective is such spam mails is to retrieve sensitive information of recipients such as their bank account numbers, passwords, and credit card credentials, privacy information etc. The Spam Emails are causing losses to business usually in billions of dollars.

"The Spam is an Unsolicited, unwanted email that was sent indiscriminately, directly, or indirectly, by a sender having no current relationship with the recipient [1]."

Let's discuss the primary motivation of spamming companies which are generating these spam emails or messages in order to deliver such information to some targeted recipient. such spam messages contains a multimedia message for advertising usually illegal or worthless products, or may be may be promoting some event, or just propagating some computer malware which is designed to hijack the spam recipient's computer. These spam messages are quite cheap to send such information's and even if one in a thousand spam recipient will respond to such messages, the spam sender will be in huge profit.[2].

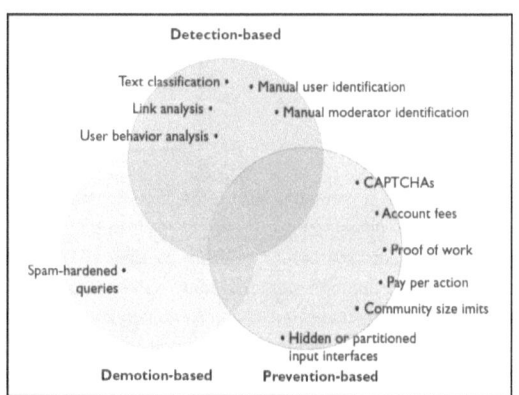

Fig. 1. Anti-Spam strategies- Detection –based, Demotion-based and Prevention based strategies. [4]

The Spam filtering is an automated technique to identity SPAM and Non-Spam also known as HAM. Generally on the basis of message contents Spam filter is taking its decision about SPAM / HAM, on basis of sender and receiver's characteristics. Spam filters are having knowledge or experience that if other users have reported similar messages as Spam or not. Such Spam filters are not so perfect, like us, therefore we need to change the working of Spam Filters by adding some more constraints to their techniques.

The Anti-Spam strategies can be categorized as follows: Detection based anti-spam strategies attempts to identify spam and remove it or reduce its prominence; where Demotion based anti-spam strategies attempts to lower the ranking of spam in ordered lists; where Prevention based strategies attempts to make contribution of spam more difficult by changing interfaces or limiting user actions.

Let's try to find out what Spammers are getting as an incentive for which they are deploying spam-bots and other such systems to generate spam messages. These incentives are listed as:

❖ In order to improve page-rankings of target websites on different search engines by sending spam emails which are containing the hyperlinks of target websites;

❖ In order to advertise some product or services or events on internet by sending bulk emails to large number of recipients;

❖ In order to record recipients contact information's and financial credentials like Date of Birth, Bank Account Number, Credit Card details, etc;

❖ In order to spread just malicious code through spam web pages;

❖ In order to destroy the website security and integrity;

❖ In order to corrupt the results of Online Voting Systems;

As per www.securelist.com the website of Kaspersky Securitylist, in year 2013 the spam statistics were as follows [12]:

❖ India is the 5th top most country at highest risk and vulnerability level [12].

❖ The Spam proportion in email was just 69.6% in 2013, which is 2.5% lesser than that in year 2012.

❖ The malicious attachments in spam emails was only 3.2% which is 0.2% lesser than that in year 2012.

❖ The phishing attacks on social networks and social websites was 32.1%

❖ India is one of the top 20 countries with 41.90% unique web users and reported is at the highest risk of computer infection through Internet.

❖ China is the largest spam populating country in 2013 with 23% of total Spam produced.

❖ About 74.5% of spam emails sent were less than 1 KB in size in 2013.

The total number of online attacks launched from different web resources worldwide increased to about 1 700 870 654 in yr 2013 as compared to 1 595 587 670 attacks reported in yr 2012 by Kaspersky Online Security products.

167

## II. PREVIOUS RESEARCH WORKS

Spam Producer companies are using automated applications to send bulk emails since mid 1990s using mail replay servers and free fake domains [7]. In the year 1994, the Canter and Siegel Company have hired a programmer just to automate posting spam messages to every existing USENET newsgroups, and they have promoted advertisement to apply for the green-card lottery. This automated software was soon evolved as the first automated bulk emailing software [9]. In the year 1995, "Floodgate" was evolved as the first commercial application to produce spam emails, and it was available to purchase at the cost of $100. Floodgate have advertised that it is going to gather the active email addresses through email address harvesting from every possible sources including newsgroups, AOL directory, CompuServe classifieds and others. After some time FloodGate have included expert additional software "Goldrush" with an ability to send out thousands of emails per hour [9]. Such software has enabled spammers to send email at a cost as low as $0.0001 per message. Since then, the spammers are playing a Tom and Jerry game with email service providers [7].

Now a day's the Mallom technology is one of the leader of anti-spam services. Mallom has defined one extra classes of spam, 'unsure' other than 'spam' and 'ham'. The Mollom is finalizing any message to be as 'spam' only when Mallom is 100% sure that the message contains some spam data and then Mallom discard any such spam posts. When Mollom is 100% sure that some message is non-spam or ham, then only this post is accepted.

Such area of uncertainty about a post is termed as a gray zone by Mallom logic and then only it gives a CAPTCHAs challenge to the user. Now such post can only be accepted when user will give correct CAPTCHA response, and the submitting entity is accepted as a human. Every other post with incorrect CAPTCHA response will be rejected by Mallom. The primary aim of Mallom is to produce CAPTCHAs to the Spambots not to the humans at all. [10]

Spam reports of SecureList [14] has suggested that Spammers are sending Holiday Spam messages to offer cheap holidays, messages to provide language learning, offers to save expenses on telephones by promoting Online Calling and SMS.

Spam reports by Symantec in November 2014[15] have shown that Kelihos is the top most Botnets with 19.2% share of Spam data, Gamut botnet is sharing 18.8% share, Snowshoe is having a share of 8.0%. One more alarming observations is that more than 41% of emails are containing links to either malicious or some compromised websites.

### III. STUDY METHODOLOGY

**We have designed our study on two aspects:** Technical standards to filter a Spam and Behavioral mindset of Spamming Bots. The CAPTCHA service is used to detect Spams bots in most of web forms. The Programmers are also using a hidden field in contact/feedback forms as a hidden Honeypot. All the spam filter applications are using Spamsets collected by different Anti-Spam organizations in order to generate a black list of IP addresses, email addresses, URL's etc.

For our studies we have used an API developed in PHP/MySQL to collect spam and ham data to demonstrate the working of our proposed spam filter.

The CAPTCHA challenge is not a challenge any more with budding solutions for automatic CAPTCHA solving. Bypass CAPTCHA (*www.bypasscaptcha.com*), CAPTCHA Brotherhood (*www.captchabrotherhood.com*), Image Decoders (*www.imagedecoders.com*), Imagetyperz (*www.imagetyperz.com*), are some of the examples of the CAPTCHA solving services, they are not using any image recognition techniques but they have deployed humans to solve these CAPTCHA puzzles. With their economical working model they have plenty of online users to solve the CAPTCHA puzzles 24 X 7.

Many programmers and Spam Filters are nowadays using a hidden Honeypot with a hidden form field managed using Java Script or CSS scripts. Such empty hidden fields are not visible therefore none of the user is going to fill this field. But the spam bots simply don't care about this hidden property as they work on the coding side. Spam bots fills this hidden field with some junk value. At the time of posting the form data, value of this hidden field is

169

compared with a null value, if any value is found in this field, presence of the spam bot is confirmed.

"Web spam detection can be viewed as a binary classification problem, where a classifier is used to predict whether a given web page or entire web site is spam or not. The machine learning community has produced a large number of classification algorithms, several of which have been used in published research on web spam detection, including decision-tree based classifiers, SVM-based classifiers, Bayesian classifiers, and logistic regression classifiers. Many spam detection techniques have been proposed in recent years. Some methods were developed through competitions such as Web Spam Challenge and Discovery Challenge"[3]. The Web spam filters can be classified into following two types: Content based spam filters and List based spam filters.

### (I.)The Content Based Spam Filters

#### A. Word-Based Filters:

The word-based spam filters are the simplest content-based spam filter. The word-based filters are simply blocking any incoming emails that contain certain listed terms or words which are extracted from spam emails in past. Since many spam messages contain some words which are no often found in personal or business communications, these word based spam filters can be a simple yet capable filtering technique for blocking spam emails. However, if we configure such filter to filter emails containing more common words, these filters may generate false positives results. These filters needs regular updates as spammers may purposefully misspell keywords to spoof word-based filters.

#### B. Heuristic Filters:

Heuristic filters are considering multiple terms contained in an email. Heuristic filters are not only scanning words or phrases in incoming emails, but all the suspicious words common in spam messages, such as "!!!" or "$$$" or "100% Free" or "Act Now!" or "Rolex" or "Viagra"[13] receive higher ranking points, on the other hand frequent terms which are found in normal emails receive lower scores. If a legitimate contact will send you such email with such words or phrases having higher spam ranking then this email will also be considered as a spam. Such emails will be considered as false positive. Spammers are learning such words and phrases and avoiding them in spam emails.

### C. Bayesian Filters:

The Bayesian filters are presently the most advanced form of content-based spam filters by using mathematical probability rules to differentiate spam and ham. Such filters get trained by end users by categorizing each email as spam or ham. As the end users starts working by keep marking emails as spam/ham over a time such filter makes a list of legitimate email senders and list of spam words and phrases. Such Bayesian filter constantly builds its list of spam words, so it's turning more and more powerful as much as it will be used. For example if "Rolex" has appeared 62 times in spam emails over a time and appeared 03 times in ham emails then there is 95% possibility that any incoming email containing "Rolex" is a spam.

### (II.)List Based Spam Filters

List-based web spam filters can detect spam mails without analyzing page contents. Trust Ranks[11] can minimize the spam pages impact on page ranking. The lists are as follows:

### A. Blacklist:

The Blacklist are list of email addresses or IP Addresses which are observed as involved in spreading and spam-filtered in order to block spam messages from this list.

**B. Real-Time Black hole List:**

This spam-filtering technique is almost same as above mentioned blacklists and they don't require much maintenance of blacklists. This spam filter needs to connect to some external list to check if sender's email or IP address is present or not.

**C. White list:**

A White list also supports spam filters by specifying the list of legitimate email or IP addresses. The spam filters may trust this White list. Spammers may spoof these addresses to send spam.

**IV. SPAM STATISTICS**

The Srizbi or Cbeplay or Exchanger botnet, is the world's topmost botnet as per the spam experts. It was sharing 60% share in the total spam being sent by other botnets combined. The Srizbi was supposed to be hosted on McColo ISP, San Jose. When this ISP was turned down in 2008 with complaints of Spamming, the global spam volume came down by 75%. Let's check the statistical data of Spam generated by Srizbi Spambot:

❖ Per day Spam Messages generated by Srizbi: 60 billion = 60 x 1,000,000,000 messages

❖ Per Second Spam Messages from Srizbi: (60 billion /24 hrs)/60mins= 694444.44444

❖ Above statistics shows that only Srizbi botnet was generating approximately 7,00,000 Spam email messages per second.

❖ If an average size of Spam email with some pictures and text is approx 10 kb

❖ Then, Srizbi server needs approx 7 Gbps bandwidth to generate Spam emails,

❖ Over a Dedicated Leased Line Internet connection with 1 : 1 Upload and download ratio, with some 10 % fluctuations in bandwidth they need a minimum of 14+1.4 = 15.4 GBps bandwidth connection.

- According to BSNL India website, *http://www.bsnl.co.in/opencms/bsnl/ BSNL/services/broadband/internet_tariff1.html,*
- We need bandwidth worth Rs. 73,12,50,000 per year to generate this much spam.

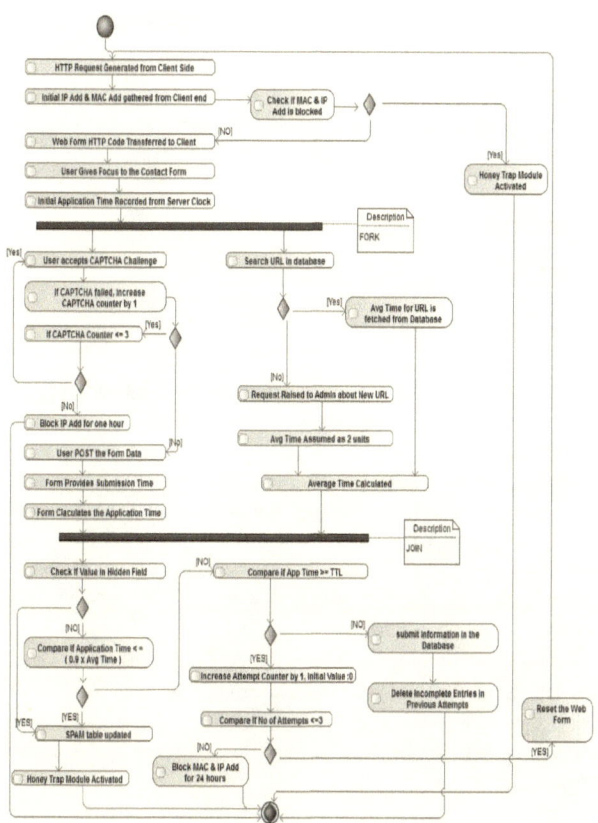

Now in place of 7,00,000 Spam emails per second, if we can restrict Srizbi server to send only 03 Spam email per minute per server at an average of 20 sec limit to fill and post a web form , and suppose we are having about 100 target servers, then Spam Emails generated comes out to be :

7,00,000 / (20 * 100) = 350 emails per second per server

"Now the ratio of spam reduction can become 99.95%"

This spam reduction ratio is inversely proportional both to the number of target servers and the minimum average time of form submission.

## V. EXPERIMENTAL SETUP

### Approach-1: Alternative use of Honeypot

Honeypot is gererally used to attract a spammer's Spam bot, in this paper we have proposed a different approach for Honeypot, referred as "HoneyTrap" now on.

Once a spam attack is diagnosed from our Spamizer algorithm, then in spite of showing a warning message to spammer "Access Denied", we will en route this spam attack to a similar application path, a Honeypot, where Spammer's Spambot will feel no difference than the actual application. But the junk contents will not be recoded in the database, and no spam email will generate, still spam bot will receive a message that spammer's "Data is successfully saved". This will not annoy the Spammer and it will keep trying sending spam. This approach will save a considerable amount of spam generated.

A HoneyPot trap or Honeytrap is a technique to detect unauthorized spam attacks by spambots to trick and reveal their identities. As all the legitimate request are sent to main server, the service degradation on Honeypot servers can be regarded due to spam and DDOS attacks by spammers.[5][6]

We are transferring the Spam Bots to Honey Trap Server when they are trying to come again by using same IP Address which we have maintained in our IP Blacklist.

**Approach-2: Spam Prevention using Hidden Form Field**

It is not possible for a Spambot to distinguish between optional or mandatory web form fields, therefore a spambot just fill every field on a web form. Every website is having different style to mark such mandatory fields, someone them are using asterisks on such required fields, some are using red colored fonts, some are using HTML5 attribute "required", and some don't bother at all to mark such fields, but they redirect you back to the web form if you have missed one such field.

Spambots always struggles to recognize required fields, and most of them also struggle to read CSS or JavaScripts on a webpage. One simple solution is to add a completely junk field in every web form and then to hide this field using CSS or Java Scripts. For example:

**<input type = "some text" name= "secret" style = "display:none;">**

You may make it more complex by giving the field a fleid ID or a class name which would then force the bot to scan through your CSS files to determine the element's visibility [7].

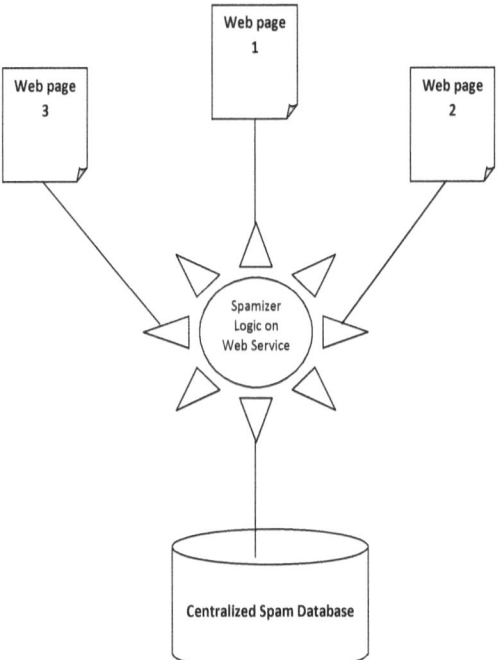

Fig. 2. Spamizer Block Diagram- We have implemented Spamizer as a Web Service which is managing number of contact forms on different web pages

**Approach-3:  Change  in Initial & Final IP Addresses**

Our Spamizer service is checking the Initial IP Address from where the HTTP request was received with the Final IP Address from where user is Posting the form data. If these addresses are not matching then there may be Spam attack. As it practically not possible to switch IP address within 10-15 seconds.

**Approach-4: Timing difference of HTTP Request and POST**

In this approach for Spam Detection, we are recording the 1st Time Stamp when user starts working on a Form, then we are recording the final Time Stamp when user submits a Form

**Application Time = Submit Time – Initial Time**

There is a Min. Submit Time of every URL containing a Contact Form, stored in a table by the admin, which we can retrieve in parallel while user is filling the form.

**If ( Application Time < = (90/100) * Minimum Submit Time )**

Then, It is an entry which can be done only using a Spam Bot, so HoneyTrap module will handle it. Update the Black List of IP Address.

Else, It is a legitimate entry and it can be stored in Database.

We are using a PHP/MySQL API for our experiment. We are using a PHP class to handle all the methods and to manage our parallel algorithm. While user was entering the form data, the parallel methods will calculate the Spam Criteria in the background. This will save the time complexity and extra payload. A single php class can manage number of web forms. We can replicate the class over a distributed system to handle the extra payload.

## VI. RESULTS

The proposed solution is implemented as an application and presently hosted on *www.manishsaxena.in/webform/contact.php*

On the basis of given formula, following are the observed values:

**If [Application_Time] < =**
**[(Min. Application_Time * Reduction Percentage)]**
**then, "Spam Attempt"**

Table I.  Observed Spam Statistics

| S. No | No. of Attempts | Reduction Factor as Percentage | No of Spam Emails | False Positive |
|-------|-----------------|-------------------------------|-------------------|----------------|
| 1. | 1000 | 90 % | 06 | 04 |
| 2. | 1000 | 80 % | 02 | NIL |
| 3. | 1000 | 50% | NIL | NIL |
| 4. | 1000 | 4 Seconds | NIL | NIL |

**The key findings of this experiment are as follows:**

❖ During application training we have observed that no human can fill up a form in less than Min. Application Time.

❖ If we have given 90 % relaxation in Min. Application Time during 1000 online attempts, 06 spam messages recorded, out of which 04 messages were false positive, which was recorded because user have opted auto-fill property in their browsers.

❖ If we have given 80 % relaxation in Min. Application Time during 1000 online attempts, 02 spam messages were recorded, out of which None was false positive, which was recorded. Here user have opted auto-form filler application such as RoboForm9.

❖ If we have given 50 % relaxation in Min. Application Time during 1000 online attempts, NONE spam messages was recorded. May be even after auto-form filler application user has to take a CAPTCHA challenge.

❖ If we have taken 04 seconds as Min. Application Time again NONE spam messages was recorded. Now only some real spam bot application can submit a form within this much time. Even they have to deploy  human by some trick to accept the CAPTCHA challenge.

❖ These results support the hypothesis that CAPTCHA is not the ultimate solution of user authentication, as it can be easily compromised by online users of CAPTCHA solving companies. So we need a solution for such companies.

❖ We are working on a new technique to generate a smart CAPTCHA to overcome such challenges.
❖ New Server technologies need to include Anti-spamming techniques and smarter Intrusion Prevention Systems to handle the SPAM attacks.
❖ By hitting the economic model of Spammers we can prevent Spamming up to a great extent.

## VII. LIMITATIONS OF THE CURRENT WORK

Though we have tested our research idea online on a shared hosting instance on a personal domain, but once it will be implemented on the real production web server on some high search ranking website, it will face an encounter by major Spam bots. We have observed that because of different security and firewall solutions our application was sometimes not able to fetch the MAC address from the user end. We are working to access MAC and IP addresses in all the cases to keep track of the suspicious users which keep changing their IP addresses to prevent their locations. If users will switch of their JavaScript's from the browsers one of our security level will suffer.

## VIII. CONCLUSION AND FUTURE SCOPE

We have suggested a multilevel approach to restrict the Web Spam in this paper. Out of given approaches, if on the basis of Application Time criteria, spam bots will definitely try to compromise the anti-spam security standards used in our approach, still if we can restrict them from sending 7L spam messages to 350 spam messages per second as proposed, it will still be a success. We are planning to add more security levels to this solution in coming time. We are in process to make a new CAPTCHA which will further reduce the spam message generation, which can easily compromise the treats of CAPTCHA solving companies. We are also planning for a Browser Plug-in to easily access the MAC Addresses from client end to add more security.

179

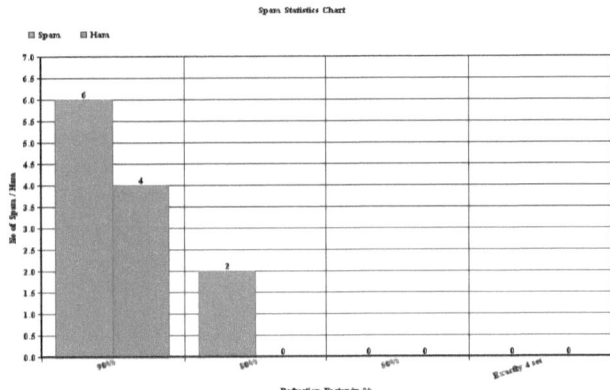

**Spam Statistics Chart**

**ACKNOWLEDGEMENT**

At the outset, authors are thankful to the Almighty God who is the most beneficent, most merciful for all his blessings, without which it wouldn't have been possible to complete this work. Authors would also like to express sincere thanks to all the peers, colleagues and organizations who supported this research by sharing their valuable time, resources and timely feedback as and when required during the course of this research work.

**REFERENCES**

**Journal References**

1. G. V. Cormack and T. R. Lynam, "TREC 2005 Spam Track Overview," *http://plg.uwaterloo.ca/~gvcormac/trecspamtrack05*, 2005.
2. M. Mangalindan, "For bulk E-mailer, pestering millions offers path to profit," Wall Street Journal, November 13, 2002.
3. G. Salton, A. Wong, and C. S. Yang. "A vector space model for automatic indexing". Commun. ACM, Vol.18, Nov. 1975.

4. Paul Heymann, Georgia Koutrika and Hector Garcia-Molina, "Fighting Spam on Social Websites: A Survey of Approaches and Future Challenges" IEEE Transactions, November 2007.

5. Manish Saxena, Mohd. Jameel Hashmi and Dr. Rajesh Saini, "Classification of DDoS Attacks and their Defense Techniques using Intrusion Prevention System", IJCSCN, ISSN No: 2249-5789, Vol.2(5), pg 607-614, October 2012.

6. Manish Saxena, Prof. Dr. Dhirendra B.Singh and Mohd. Jameel Hashmi, "Intrusion Prevention System based defense techniques to manage DDoS Attacks", TIJCSA, ISSN No: 2278-1080, Vol.1(8), October 2012.

7. Goodman, Joshua, Gordon V. Cormack, and David Heckerman. 2007. "Spam and the Ongoing Battle for the Inbox." Communications of the ACM 50(2): 24–33.

**Web References**

1. Sitepoint, "Easy Spam Prevention Using Hidden Form Fields";

2. *http://www.sitepoint.com/easy-spam-prevention-using-hidden-form-fields/*

3. Zdziarski, Jonathan A. 2005. Ending Spam:Bayesian Content Filtering and the Art of Statistical Language Classifi cation. No Starch Press.

4. Mollom, "Mollom Technical Whitepaper", *https://mollom.com/files/mollom-technical-whitepaper.pdf*

5. Zhai. "Statistical Language Models for Information Retrieval". Now Publishers Inc., Hanover, MA, 2008.

6. Kaspersky Securitylist 2013, *www.securitylist.com*,

7. CallidusCloud, Lead Views,

8. *"http://www.leadformix.com/blog/2013/09/top-100-spam-trigger-words-and-phrases-to-avoid/"*

9. Monthly SPAM report of SecureList.com, March 2014 *http://securelist.com/analysis/monthly-spam-reports/59420/ spam-report-march-2014/*

10. Symantec Security Response Publications, November 2014, *http://www.symantec.com/security_response/publications/monthlythreatreport.jsp*

**Annexure – II :**
Handling CAPTCHA free web-form spam with Spamizer' 1.1
Proceedings of the 11th INDIACom; INDIACom-2017
4th International Conference on "Computing for Sustainable Global Development", 01st – 03rd March, 2017

# HANDLING CAPTCHA FREE WEB-FORM SPAM WITH SPAMIZER'1.1

Dr. Manish Saxena
Department of MCA,
FGIET, Raebareli, U.P.
India
Email: gmail@manish
saxena.in

Prof.(Dr.) Usman Ali Khan
Department of Info.
Systems,
KAA University, Jeddah,
Saudi Arabia
Email:
usmansaysto@gmail.com

Hemant Kumar Singh
Department of MCA,
FGIET, Raebareli, U.P.
India
Email: hemantmca1.imr
@gmail.com

**Abstract –** The Unsolicited Bulk Email (UBE) or SPAM are regularly causing potential losses to online business and email account holders. The conventional Spam filtering is purely based on automatically identifying SPAM and HAM (Non-Spam). The CATPCHA is one of the popular techniques to detect Web Spamming, which is increasing the complexity of form submission by even the genuine or HAM users. In this research work, we tried to skip filling CAPTCHA and still managing to control the SPAM by a significant margin. We have proposed a modified algorithm for Spam Filtering in which behavioral approach of Spammers is considered to restrict the grown of economical status of Spam generating companies. We have used a special hidden Honeytrap module to minimize the spam generation by the Web forms available on various public and social networking websites for comment, feedback or contact.

**Keywords** – Spamizer, Spam bots, Spamizer'1.1, CAPTCHA, HoneyTrap, Comment Spam.

## NOMENCLATURE

SPAM – Unsolicited, Unwanted Email

HAM – Non spam Message

UBE – Unsolicited Bulk Email

CAPTCHA – A spam detecting technique which means "Completely Automated Public Turing test to tell Computers and Human Apart".

SPAMIZER – Name of our previously proposed algorithm.

SPAMIZER'1.1 – Name of our Newly proposed algorithm.


## I. INTRODUCTION

In the present era, electronic communications are doing Spamming by sending usually unwanted and unsolicited emails and messages in bulk quantity without the will or consent of the recipients. Such Unsolicited Bulk Emails (UBE) are also known as Spam email. Sending a Spam Email is one of the most preferred spamming types. The principal objective of spamming is to retrieve sensitive financial credential or personal information of spam-recipients, such as their bank account numbers, passwords, like their banking passwords, credit card details, privacy information, like spouse name, date of birth, photographs etc. The Spam Emails can cause losses up to billions of dollars or above.

"The Spam is an Unwanted and Unsolicited email that was sent indiscriminately, directly or indirectly, by a sender having no current relationship with the recipient [1]."

The prime motive of companies producing spam or sending spam emails on commercial basis to generate major motivation of spam producing companies is to convey such spam information to targeted recipients group. Such spam emails generally contains some Image as URL link or some multimedia message for advertising some service or products, with a motive

183

to sell generally illegal or worthless products. Such spam emails may also be promoting some future event. Spam emails also contain some malware program which is specially programmed to hijack and spam PC of the recipient's. These spam emails are so cheap in cost that even if one in a thousand recipients will purchase this product, cost of entire spamming will be covered and company will be in the huge returns n profits [2].

The Spam filtering is basically an automated process to distinguish between SPAM and HAM (Non-Spam). Usually most of the Spam filter algorithms differentiate between SPAM / HAM, on the basis of the contents of that message. This Spam filter contains sufficient knowledge and experience on the basis of user actions after reading that spam email. If user has reported as SPAM on the basis on contents, it will be recorded and further emails from same source will be sent in spam folder from the next time. This is also known as Bayesian filtering, but these Spam filters are not so perfect, therefore its required to change some working policies and techniques of Spam Filters by adding some advanced constraints.

The WWW world is changing. Now a User contribution can make or break a website. Every website is allowing users to participate and contribute with the activities or contents of that website. With this level of participation, keeping your site under control will always be a huge challenge.

We can either detect the spamming effort, which works to find and identify spam and then works to remove it in order to reduce the prominence of spam attack; or we can use a Demotion strategies of anti-spamming which works on ordered lists to lower down the spam ranking; or we can use Prevention based anti-spamming strategy which works by changing difficult interfaces for spam to attack.

The Spammers are generating spam messages or deploying the spam-bots for below mentioned incentives:

❖ Attempt to improve the page-rankings of target spam web sites on different search engines, like Google, MSN, Yahoo, etc.;
❖ Attempt to advertise certain product or some specific services or particular events on the web by sending bulk emails containing advertising links to large number of recipients;

- ❖ In order to collect the contact information's and financial details like Date of Birth, Bank Account Number, Credit Card credentials, etc of the recipients.
- ❖ In order to circulate only malicious code via spam web pages;

As per the report of Kaspersky Securitylist Network, dated 3rd Quarter on www.securelist.com in year 2016, the statistics of spam emails are as follows [13]:

- ❖ India is on the 7th rank with 24.35% attacks by mobile malware.
- ❖ According to Kaspersky Security Network data, they have detected and repelled 171,802,109 numbers of malicious attacks from various online resources from a total of 190 countries all over the world.
- ❖ Web antivirus components have recognized 45,169,524 numbers of unique URLs as malicious.
- ❖ KSN antivirus has detected 12,657,673 numbers of unique malicious scripts, exploits, executable files, etc.
- ❖ A total of 1,198,264 user computers have reported infection attempts by malware which aims to steal money from online access to their bank accounts.
- ❖ A total of 821,865 computers have reported a Crypto ransomware attacks.
- ❖ KSN antivirus has detected a total of 116,469,744 unique potentially unwanted and malicious objects.
- ❖ In 2nd Quarter of 2016, a total of 36,26,458 malicious installation packages were detected.
- ❖ DangerousObject.Multi.Generic has attacked 78.5% KSN users in Q3, 2016.
- ❖ India is in the list of **top 20 countries with highest number of unique web users.** India is also considered as highly risky nation for computer infection propagated via web because of lack of awareness and literacy rates.
- ❖ USA was reported as the Worst Spam heaven country, as they were having 3049 number of current Live Spam issues in November 2016.

- ❖ The most of spam emails were less than 1 KB in size.
- ❖ In 2015, KSN Solutions repelled approximately 800 million attacks which were launched from various online resources around the globe.
- ❖ The most of online attacks were having malicious URLs.
- ❖ In 2015, a 34.2% numbers of user computers were victim of at least one online attack.
- ❖ Russia is having largest number of unique users (48.9%) facing the highest risk of online infections.

## II. PREVIOUS RESEARCH WORKS

The Spam generating companies are using various automated applications/Trojans/spam bots in order to send bulk/spam emails. Since 1990s free fake domains and mail replay servers are used for this purpose[7]. The Canter and Siegel Company hired a programmer in year 1994 for posting automated spam messages to all the registered USENET newsgroups. Also they were promoting to apply for green-card lottery by sending advertisements. Later on, this automated software was considered as the very first automated software to send bulk emails[10]. The "Floodgate" was first commercial application evolved as an automated spam email sending software. That time it was available to procure at $100. The Floodgate have announced to gather active email addresses from email harvesting from all the possible sources, like emails, webpages, AOL directory, CompuServe classifieds, newsgroups and others. The FloodGate then started using expert additional software to send millions of emails per hour known as "Goldrush"[10]. The softwares' like FloodGate was so economically viable that it may send spam emails at merely $0.0001 per message. Then on, spammers started flooding spam emails in every active email accounts. [8].

Presently the Mollom technology is emerging as a leader in field of anti-spam services. The Mollom is basically a Web Service on Cloud (Software as a Service) which helps you to identify quality of the web or comment contents and, also helps you to spam through comments or spam generating from contact forms, The Mollom is providing top priority protection in web registration or web contact forms.

The Mollom is using a different spam class than Spam and Ham, known as 'unsure' class. The Mallom reports any email message as a 'spam' only when Mallom is 100% sure about the message is containing some spam category data. Once reporting this message as a Spam, Mollom discards all similar spam posts with such content. Any post will be accepted only when Mollom is 100% sure that some message is of ham or non-spam category.

When some post will be termed as 'unsure' then it will be considered to lie in the gray zone, because of its uncertainty factor. In this case Mollom logic gives a CAPTCHAs challenge to the user, to be sure about a non-spam message, by some human. When user will submit correct CAPTCHA response, then only this post will be accepted. Mollom will surely reject all the posts with incorrect CAPTCHA response. The primary objective Mollom is to detect the spammer and give a CAPTCHA challenge only to the Spambots and not at all to the humans.[11]

The WPBruiser which is formerly known as GoodBye Captcha, is basically an application or framework plugin, for anti-spamming and security specially used for WordPress. The WPBruiser is based on particular algorithms which can identify spam bots without using any irritating CAPTCHA images [14]. The WPBruiser are quite successful to eliminate spam-bot signups, comment spam, and even brute force attacks, after installing on a WordPress website. Any end-user cannot sense the presence of such a security plugin. Some other anti-spamming plugins detects spam comments and then move these emails to spam folder, then user has to decide to delete or not. The WPBruiser prevents the spambots from storing spam thus making your website not only spam free and faster. Also, WPBruiser is totally independent and don't need support of any outside service.

The WPBruiser can even fights with Brute Force attacks and eliminates spambots [14].

The Google uses reCAPTCHA! The new version of reCAPTCHA is available now. Now users don't need to type jumbled text or tilted numbers. A Legitimate user just need to click at the required box on the reCAPTCHA section to confirm they are not a robot. They are calling it as the No CAPTCHA reCAPTCHA experience.[15]

## III. STUDY METHODOLOGY

In our previous research we have developed a Spamizer algorithm [8], an anti-spamming algorithm which was based on two different approaches- Spam filtering Technical approach and Spam filtering on basis of behavioral aspect of various Spam Bots.

There is a technical approach to place a hidden field in web form made for contact/feedback purposes. This fields acts like a hidden Honeypot.

The CAPTCHA challenge is a popular standard to detect presence of Spam bots by giving a challenge to read some words written in a jumbled and curvy manner. Now a day's some CAPTCHA are giving visual challenges to detect some particular animal from a group of animal, or clicking on a check box type image. Usually all the Spam Bots fires multiple instances to fill same web form as they use the script-code than using a GUI of that web form.

This time we have worked on a different hypothesis, that, we can prevent web spamming even without using a CAPTCHA at all. As we believe that the CAPTCHA challenge is not a challenge any more. Many automatically CAPTCHA filling solutions are available online like what available on www.captchabrotherhood.com, www.bypasscaptcha.com etc. These solutions are based on either image recognition techniques as well as by deploying free of cost humans by some catchy tricks to solve the CAPTCHA puzzles for others. They have such a luring working model that number of online users are round-the-clock available to solve the CAPTCHA puzzles.

Almost every Anti-spam organization are collecting Spam-URL's, IP addresses and email addresses, and then generating Spamsets. Such Spamsets can be used by the other Anti-spam solutions to detect possible Spammers.

We have used an API developed in PHP/MySQL to collect different spam and ham data in order to demonstrate working of Spamizer'1.1, which is the name given to our proposed anti-spamming solution.

For the same purpose we have studied different popular spam-bots, and from their usage statistics we have formulated certain tricks to restrict the Spam-bots.

### IV. CAPTCHA Free SPAM Detection

We have studied a famous Spam-bot Srizbi aka Exchanger aka Cbeplay. Few years back, this Spam-bot was so much popular that it was single-handedly generating more than 60% of the total spam worldwide. If we can restrict any SPAM-bot of such category, which is suppose generating 7,00,000 spam emails per second. If such a spam-bot is restricted to send merely 03 Spam emails out of 7,00,000 per minute per server with an average of 20 seconds limit for its application time to fill and post a web form. If suppose a spam-bot is targeting on some 100 target servers, then Spam Emails generated in this fashion will be only '350' as per following calculation:

*7,00,000 emails / (20 sec limit x 100 target servers)*

*= 350 emails per server per second.*

**"The spam reduction ratio will be more than 99.95%"**

The spam reduction ratio is inversely proportional to the number of target servers and also inversely proportional to the minimum average form submission time.

## V. EXPERIMENTAL SETUP

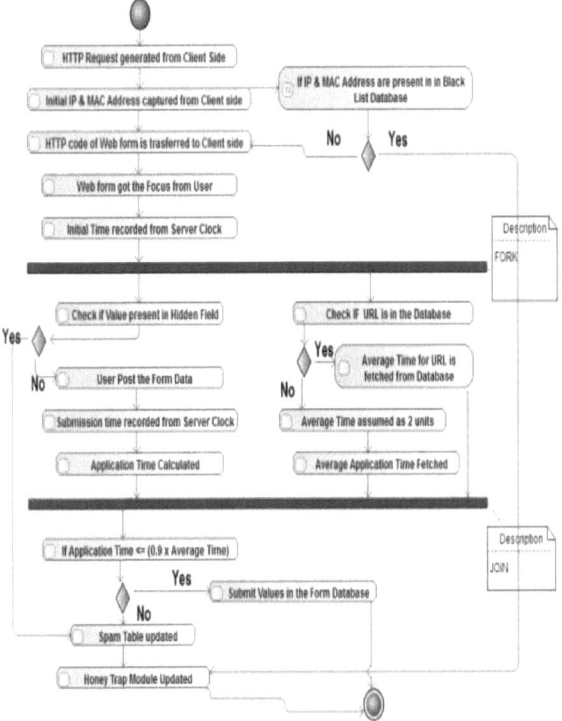

Fig. 1. Spamizer'1.1 Activity Diagram

### Stage-1: Honeypot Trap

The Honeytrap is a detection technique for spam attacks to reveal identities of spam bots. All the legitimate network traffic will be routed to the main application server, to avoid the service degradation by spam traffic or DDoS attacks. [5][6]

190

If HTTP request from Web Form is coming from such an IP address or MAC address, which is already present in the Black list as provided by Anti-Spam databases or as per Black List on our database, then such traffic from the Spam Bots will be transferred to our HoneyTrap Server.

In our research work we have used a new approach to handle the Honeypot, which we termed as "HoneyTrap". In this approach, once a traffic from spambot will be diagnosed through our Spamizer'1.1 algorithm, then we instead of showing any warning message to spammer like "Access Denied", the spam traffic will be routed to another application which is similar in looks and functionality, a Honeypot application, where a Spambot will not feel any difference as compare to the actual application. This application will make sure that there it'll not be storing any junk contents by spambots in the actual application database. Also there will not be any spam emails generated by this application. With this policy the spambot will receive a message that "Data is successfully saved". Now, Spambots will not be annoyed by any sort of warning message and spammer will be happy with the fact that spam emails are generating out of its efforts. So spammer will not try a different approach to spoof our application.

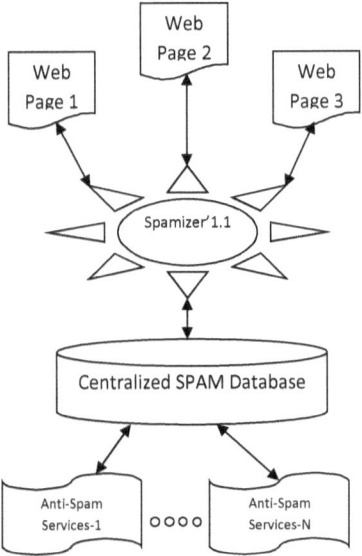

Fig. 2. Spamizer Block Diagram- We have implemented Spamizer as a Web Service which is managing number of contact forms on different web pages

**Stage-2: Hidden Form Field and Spam Prevention**

The Spambot usually fills every possible field in a web form with some junk or promotional data. The Spambots never distinguish between web form fields, if they are optional or mandatory fields. Each website is having different marking styles for such mandatory fields, some are using (*) asterisks on these fields, some use red or special colored fonts for mandatory fields, and some websites use a special HTML5 attribute termed as "required".

A Spambots cannot recognize if there are any required fields or CSS or JavaScript present on the web form. We can add an unusual text field in our web form which will be made hidden from legitimate users by a trick by using CSS / JavaScript just as follows:

<input type = "text" style = "display : none; "

name= "top_secret">

If we are using some class name or some field_ID then this will be more complex for a spambot to understand such a programming logic. The logic will be hidden in the associated CSS files to control the visibility of this hidden field. [8]

**Stage-3: HTTP Request and POST Timing difference**

We are considering two different Time stamps to detect the Spamming attempt, firstly as focus is received by the Web Form, termed as Initial time and second time POST method will be fired at the end of submission of form data, termed as Submit Time.

**Application Time = Submit Time – Initial Time**

During the training period, we record the minimum time required by the legitimate users to submit the form by entering the genuine entries, for every web page having Spamizer'1.1 logic. This Minimum Submit Time of every URL is stored in a table in the database by the administrator. This Min Application Time will be retrieved in parallel when user is filling the web form.

If the Application Time is less or equal to the 90% of Minimum Submit Time recorded during the training period, then this user may be a Spambot. Now such traffic will be handled by the HoneyTrap module so save the performance of main application server. The IP & MAC addresses have been already recorded before reaching stage, and same will be updated in Black List of IP & MAC Address. But, if the application time is well within the limits, the data will be stored in Application's Database.

We have used an API programmed with PHP and MySQL in this experiment. We have made a PHP class with certain methods and to manage the working of this parallel algorithm. We have used parallel algorithm in order to save the application time. When a user will enter data in web form, the parallel algorithm will check the spam logic in parallel, in the background.

We can save the time complexity and useless payload from the application by using such parallel logic.

## VI. RESULTS

We have implemented our proposed algorithm hosted on following URL on a shared hosting and personal URL:

*www.manishsaxena.in/webform/contact_form.php*

Based on the following formula, we have observed the spamming attempts:

**If [Application_Time] < =**

**(Minimum Application_Time x Reduction Factor as %)**

**then, "Spamming Confirmed"**

Table.1 Spam statistics as observed

| S. No. | Number of Attempts | Reduction Factor(%) | No of Spam Emails | False Positive Emails |
|--------|--------------------|--------------------|-------------------|----------------------|
| 1. | 1000 | 90 % | 06 | 04 |
| 2. | 1000 | 80 % | 02 | NIL |
| 3. | 1000 | 70% | NIL | NIL |
| 4. | 1000 | 60% | NIL | NIL |
| 5. | 1000 | 50% | NIL | NIL |
| 6. | 1000 | 40% | NIL | NIL |
| 7. | 1000 | 25% | NIL | NIL |
| 8. | 1000 | 10% | NIL | NIL |
| 9 | 1000 | 2 Seconds | NIL | NIL |

Following are some of the key findings out of our proposed algorithm to find spam attempts:

❖ While doing the training of our web application with a variety of online users, we have practically verified that it is not possible to fill up our web form in less than recorded Minimum Application Time.

❖ While giving 90% relaxation in the Minimum Application Time, out of 1000 attempts, only 06 spam messages were recorded. In which only 04 messages were false positive, which were recorded as these 04 users have used auto-fill property given in their web browsers.

❖ While giving 80% relaxation in the Minimum Application Time, out of 1000 attempts, only 02 spam messages were recorded. In which NONE were false positive, which were recorded as these 02 users have used auto-form filler application such as RoboForm9.

❖ While giving 70% relaxation in the Minimum Application Time, out of 1000 attempts, none spam or false positive messages were recorded.

❖ While giving 60% relaxation in the Minimum Application Time, out of 1000 attempts, none spam or false positive messages were recorded.

❖ While giving 50% relaxation in the Minimum Application Time, out of 1000 attempts, none spam or false positive messages were recorded.

❖ While giving 40% relaxation in the Minimum Application Time, out of 1000 attempts, none spam or false positive messages were recorded.

❖ While giving 25% relaxation in the Minimum Application Time, out of 1000 attempts, none spam or false positive messages were recorded.

❖ While giving 10% relaxation in the Minimum Application Time, out of 1000 attempts, none spam or false positive messages were recorded.

❖ While giving specifically 02 seconds as Minimum Application Time, out of 1000 attempts, none spam or false positive messages were recorded.

❖ These results support the hypothesis that we can prevent web spamming without using CAPTCHA. The CAPTCHA can be easily compromised by tricks used by CAPTCHA solving companies.

❖ If upcoming Operating Systems will include Anti-spamming techniques as proposed in this research work, then we can handle the SPAM attacks quite easily.

❖ By using proposed solution as Anti-Spamming model, we can hit the economic model of Spamming companies.

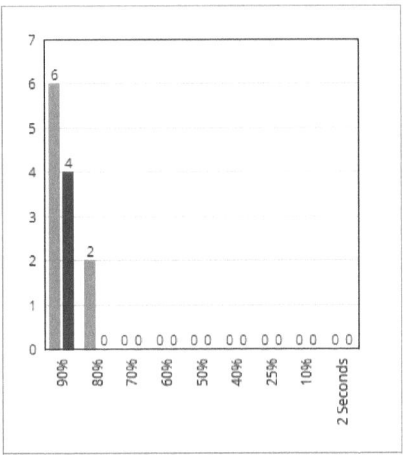

Fig.3 Graph of Spamizer'1.1 Results

## VII. LIMITATIONS

We have implemented our research idea online on my personal domain hosted on shared hosting server. Once it will be implemented on some high search ranking website like IRCTC, etc. this logic has to face major Spam bots attacks. Most of times we were not able to track the actual MAC & IP addresses of the users because of their Internet security software or Firewall solutions. If JavaScript of web browsers will be turned off, Hidden input technique will fail to provide security.

196

## VIII. CONCLUSION AND FUTURE SCOPE

In this paper, we have suggested a unique approach to handle the Web Spam. Our approach is based on multiple levels to filter out the spammer as soon as we confirm the spamming approach. In these multiple approaches, Minimum Application Time criteria cannot be compromised by the spammers because of their behavioral attitude of sending maximum possible spam emails per seconds. In this way even if we can restrict spammers sending 99.98% less spam messages per second as we have proposed, it be a grand success and their business model will be crashed. We are adding more security levels to our next version Spamizer'1.2 which is under development. We are also working on anti-spamming browsers plug-in, to restrict more spam messages.

## ACKNOWLEDGEMENT

The authors are thankful to the Almighty God, our parents, our families for all the blessings, patience and moral support to complete this research. Authors would also like to express their sincere thanks to all the colleagues for their support during the course of this research work.

## REFERENCES

### Journal References

1. G. V. Cormack and T. R. Lynam, "TREC 2005 Spam Track Overview," *http://plg.uwaterloo.ca/~gvcormac/trecspamtrack05*, 2005.

2. M. Mangalindan, "For bulk E-mailer, pestering millions offers path to profit," Wall Street Journal, November 13, 2002.

3. G. Salton, A. Wong, and C. S. Yang. "A vector space model for automatic indexing". Commun. ACM, Vol.18, Nov. 1975.

4. Paul Heymann, Georgia Koutrika and Hector Garcia-Molina, "Fighting Spam on Social Websites: A Survey of Approaches and Future Challenges" IEEE Transactions, November 2007.

5.  Manish Saxena, Mohd. Jameel Hashmi and Dr. Rajesh Saini, "Classification of DDoS Attacks and their Defense Techniques using Intrusion Prevention System", IJCSCN, ISSN No: 2249-5789, Vol.2(5), pg 607-614, October 2012.

6.  Manish Saxena, Prof. Dr. Dhirendra B.Singh and Mohd. Jameel Hashmi, "Intrusion Prevention System based defense techniques to manage DDoS Attacks", TIJCSA, ISSN No: 2278-1080, Vol.1(8), October 2012.

7.  Goodman, Joshua, Gordon V. Cormack, and David Heckerman. 2007. "Spam and the Ongoing Battle for the Inbox." Communications of the ACM 50(2): 24–33.

8.  Manish Saxena, P.M. Khan, "Spamizer : An approach to handle web form spam", INDIACom-2015, 2nd IEEE sponsored, International Conference on "Computing for Sustainable Global Development", 11th – 13th March, 2015, BVICAM, New Delhi (INDIA)

**Web References**

1.  Sitepoint, "Easy Spam Prevention Using Hidden Form Fields";

2.  *http://www.sitepoint.com/easy-spam-prevention-using-hidden-form-fields/*

3.  Zdziarski, Jonathan A. 2005. Ending Spam:Bayesian Content Filtering and the Art of Statistical Language Classifi cation. No Starch Press.

4.  Mollom, "Mollom Technical Whitepaper", *https://mollom.com/files/mollom-technical-whitepaper.pdf*

5.  Zhai. "Statistical Language Models for Information Retrieval". Now Publishers Inc., Hanover, MA, 2008.

6.  Kaspersky Securitylist 2016, *www.securitylist.com*,

7.  WPBruiser {no- Captcha anti-Spam}, *https://wordpress.org/plugins/goodbye-captcha/*

8.  Introducing the new reCAPTCHA, *https://www.google.com/recaptcha/intro/index.html*

Annexure - III

ISSN 2250-0987

Manish Saxena, UNIASCIT, Vol 3 (1), 2013, 347-352

# NETWORK INTRUSION PREVENTION SYSTEM TECHNIQUES TO MANAGE DDOS ATTACKS

**Manish Saxena**

Asst. Professor, MCA Dept, FGIET, Raebareli, India

**Abstract:** Nowadays, guarantee of secure communication is as important as the traditional computer and information security assurance. Presently Distributed Denial of Service (DDoS) Attacks are causing billions of dollars losses by affecting the normal functioning of organizations. DDoS attackers are infiltrating large numbers of computers by exploiting software vulnerabilities. By the time specific countermeasures are developed to prevent DDoS attacks, attackers enhance existing DDoS attack tools, developing new and derivative DDoS attack tools and techniques. Organizations are trying their best to minimize their losses from these systems. However, most of the organizations widely use the Intrusion Prevention Systems (IPS) to observe and manage their networks. In this paper the Preventive, Detective and Mitigation DDoS Defence techniques and Mechanisms have been discussed to strengthen existing IPS concepts, which can help to develop a new and intelligent Network Intrusion Prevention System. A new technique for an intelligent and smart Intrusion Prevention system has been introduced on the basis of Captcha, IP addresses, MAC Addresses and Application_Id.

**Keywords-** DDoS, Intrusion Prevention System, Preventive, Detective & Mitigation Techniques, Application_Id.

## 1. Introduction

Prevention of illegitimate traffic is one of the goals of communication security and seeks to prevent an eavesdropper from gaining any meaningful information about network users' behavior or objectives by observing the legitimate traffic on the network. Denial of service attacks have become a growing problem over the last few years resulting in large losses for the victims [2]. One good example of this loss is the attacks of Yahoo, CNN, and Amazon in February of 2000 which had an estimated loss of several million to over a billion dollars [8]. This paper will discuss the concepts of denial of service attacks, how they can be detected, and some of the most common ways of mitigating the damage they can inflict upon their victims.

Distributed Denial of Service (DDoS) attacks are a virulent, frequent type of attack on the availability of Internet services and resources. DDoS attackers infiltrate large numbers of computers by exploiting software vulnerabilities, to set up DDoS attack networks. These unwitting computers are then invoked to wage a coordinated, large-scale attack against one or more victim systems. As specific countermeasures are developed, attackers enhance existing DDoS attack tools, developing new and derivative DDoS techniques and attack tools. Rather than react to new attacks with specific countermeasures, it would be desirable to develop comprehensive DDoS solutions that defend against known and future DDoS attack variants. However, this requires a comprehensive understanding of the scope and techniques used in different DDoS attacks.

After this introduction part rest of the paper is organized as follows: Investigation of DDoS attack problem is given in Section 2; DDoS Attack Defence Mechanisms have been proposed in Section 3; Proposed Intrusion Prevention System has been given in Section 4; Related work has been discussed in Section 5 and paper is finally concluded in Section 6.

## 2. Materials and Methods

### 2.1 DDoS Attacks

A DDoS attack can be characterized by an explicit attempt of attackers to prevent legitimate users of a service from using that service. E.g. :

- ❖ Attempts to "flood" a network, thereby preventing legitimate network traffic
- ❖ Attempts to disrupt connections between two machines, thereby preventing access to a service
- ❖ Attempts to prevent a particular individual from accessing a service
- ❖ Attempts to disrupt service to a specific system or person

Distributed denial of service attacks are basically denial of service attacks perpetrated by many systems at the same time on a single victim. Such an attack occurs in two phases, the recruiting stage where the attacker recruits machines infecting them with an attack code and the actual attack phase when the recruited machines run the attack code [14]. Some tools used by attackers in the past have included Trinoo (Trojan horse first discovered on December 30th 1999) [5], Tribe Flood Network (capable of UDP, ICMP, SYN Flood attacks as well as Smurf attacks) [3] and stacheldraht (based on Tribe Flood Network's Code) [4].

Denial-of-service attacks come in a variety of forms and aim at a variety of services. There are three basic types of attack:

- ❖ consumption of scarce, limited, or non-renewable resources
- ❖ destruction or alteration of configuration information
- ❖ physical destruction or alteration of network components

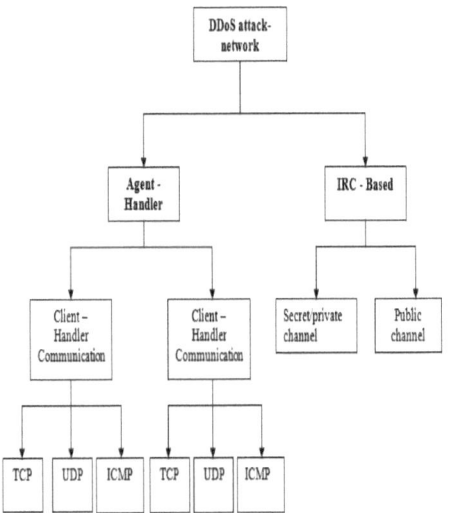

Fig 1 : DDoS Attack Network [6]

Distributed denial of service attacks can be deeply analyzed and broken into a variety of components [1]. Figure 1 shows two main types of DDoS attack networks: the Agent-Handler model and the Internet Relay Chat (IRC-Based) model.

## 2.1 Agent-Handler Model

An Agent-Handler DDoS attack network consists of clients, handlers, and agents (Figure 2). The client platform is where the attacker communicates with the rest of the DDoS attack network. The handlers are software packages located on computing systems throughout the Internet that the attacker uses to communicate indirectly with the agents. The agent software exists in compromised systems that will eventually carry out the attack on the victim system.

The attacker communicates with any number of handlers to identify which agents are up and running, when to schedule attacks, or when to upgrade agents. Depending on how the attacker configures the DDoS attack network, agents can be instructed to communicate with a single handler or multiple handlers. The communication between attacker and handler and between the handler and agents can be via TCP, UDP, or ICMP protocols. Sometimes handler and agents are known as master and daemons. The systems that have been violated to run the agent software are referred to as the secondary victims, while the target of the DDoS attack is called the (primary) victim.

## 2.2 IRC Based Attack Models

Internet Relay Chat (IRC) is a multi-user, on-line chatting system. It allows computer users to create two-party or multi-party interconnections and type messages in real time to each other [9]. IRC chat networks allow their users to create public, private and secret channels. Public channels are channels where multiple users can chat and share messages and files. [10]. Private and secret channels are set up by users to communicate with only other designated users. Both private and secret channels protect the names and messages of users that are logged on from users who do not have access to the channel [11].

An IRC-Based DDoS attack network is similar to the Agent-Handler DDoS attack model except that instead of using a handler program installed on a network server, an IRC communication channel is used to connect the client to the agents. By making use of an IRC channel, attackers using this type of DDoS attack architecture have additional benefits. For example, attackers can use "legitimate" IRC ports for sending commands to the agents [12]. The agent software installed in the IRC network usually communicates to the IRC channel and notifies the attacker when the agent is up and running.

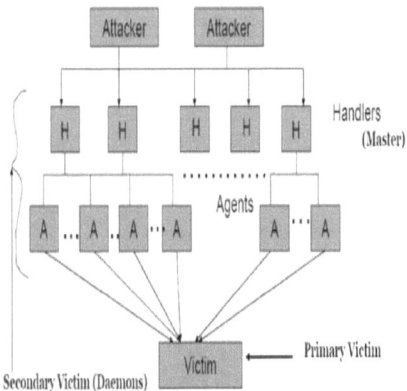

Fig 2: Agent-Handler Model

In an IRC-based DDoS attack architecture, the agents are often referred to as "Zombie Bots" or "Bots". In both IRC-based and Agent-Handler DDoS attack models, we will refer to the agents as "secondary victims" or "zombies."

### 2.3 Common Facilitation Characteristics

The hackers are using following common programs in order to facilitate DDoS attacks:

**Trinoo**

Communication between clients, handlers and agents use ports, which are default ports for this tool :

**1524 tcp**

**27665 tcp**

**27444 udp**

**31335 udp**

**TFN**

Communication between clients, handlers and agents use :

**ICMP ECHO and**

**ICMP ECHO REPLY packets.**


**Stacheldraht**

Communication between clients, handlers and agents use these ports:

**16660 tcp**

**65000 tcp**

**ICMP ECHO**

**ICMP ECHO REPLY**

**TFN2K**

Communication between clients, handlers and agents does not use any specific port, for example, it may be supplied on run time or it is chosen randomly by a program, but is a combination of

UDP,

ICMP and

TCP packets.

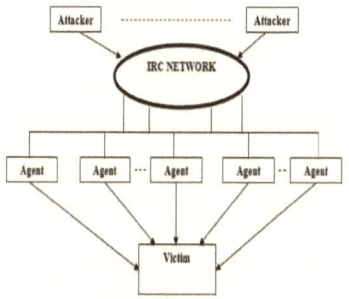

Fig 3: IRC Based Attack Model

### 3. DDoS Attack Defence Mechanisms

The seriousness of the DDoS problem and the increased frequency of DDoS attacks have led to the advent of numerous DDoS defence mechanisms. Some of these mechanisms address a specific kind of DDoS attack such as attacks on Web servers or authentication servers. Other approaches attempt to solve the entire generic DDoS problem. Based on the activity level of DDoS defence mechanisms, we differentiate between preventive and reactive mechanisms.

3.1 Preventive Mechanisms

The goal of preventive mechanisms is either to eliminate the possibility of DDoS attacks altogether or to enable potential victims to endure the attack without denying services to legitimate clients. According to these goals we further divide preventive mechanisms into attack prevention and denial-of-service prevention mechanisms.

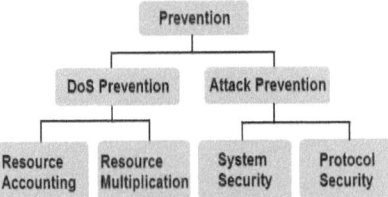

Fig 4: DDoS Prevention Defence Mechanisms.

We encourage you to consider the following options with respect to your needs:

❖ Implement router filters as described in [15]. This will lessen your exposure to certain denial-of-service attacks. Additionally, it will aid in preventing users on your network from effectively launching certain denial-of-service attacks.

- ❖ If they are available for your system, install patches to guard against TCP SYN flooding as described in [15]. This will substantially reduce your exposure to these attacks but may not eliminate the risk entirely.
- ❖ Disable any unused or unneeded network services. This can limit the ability of an intruder to take advantage of those services to execute a denial-of-service attack.
- ❖ Enable quota systems on your operating system if they are available. For example, if your operating system supports disk quotas, enable them for all accounts, especially accounts that operate network services. In addition, if your operating system supports partitions or volumes (i.e., separately mounted file systems with independent attributes) consider partitioning your file system so as to separate critical functions from other activity.
- ❖ Observe your system performance and establish baselines for ordinary activity. Use the baseline to gauge unusual levels of disk activity, CPU usage, or network traffic.
- ❖ Routinely examine your physical security with respect to your current needs. Consider servers, routers, unattended terminals, network access points, wiring closets, environmental systems
- ❖ such as air and power, and other components of your system.
- ❖ Use Tripwire or a similar tool to detect changes in configuration information or other files.
- ❖ Invest in and maintain "hot spares" - machines that can be placed into service quickly in the event that a similar machine is disabled.
- ❖ Invest in redundant and fault-tolerant network configurations.
- ❖ Establish and maintain regular backup schedules and policies, particularly for important configuration information.
- ❖ Establish and maintain appropriate password policies, especially access to highly privileged accounts such as UNIX root or Microsoft Windows NT Administrator. [7]

## 3.2 Detective Mechanisms

Reactive mechanisms strive to alleviate the impact of an attack on the victim. In order to attain this goal they need to detect the attack and respond to it. The goal of attack detection is to detect every attempted DDoS attack as early as possible and to have a low degree of false positives. Upon attack detection, steps can be taken to characterize the packets belonging to the attack stream and provide this characterization to the response mechanism.

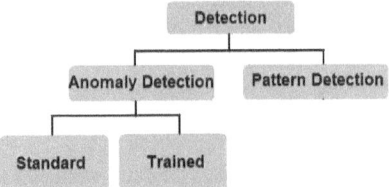

Fig 5: DDoS Detection Defence Mechanisms.

## 3.3 Mitigation Mechanisms

When a customer or the network infrastructure is under attack, monitoring is important for quick identification of the attack characteristics and entry points but the next question that immediately follows is, "What are you going to do to stop it?" Good mitigation techniques are a required part of a service provider's security architecture.

### 3.3.1 ACLs/Rate Limiting

Access control lists (ACL) or firewall filters are the first line of defence for a service provider. For a simple DDoS attack directed at a single customer, deployment of an egress ACL on the customer's edge router is an easy way to stop the attack. The problem with this technique is scaling both from a router performance perspective and as the number of attacks managed increases.

Operation personnel deploying the ACLs must know the performance limitation of the routers they are using. ASIC based ACLs will perform better than

ACLs processed in software. Different ASICs can and do have different performance characteristics based on the packet size, interface speed and other features turned on in the router and interface cards. Most service providers have home grown scripts for their router configuration and ACL management.

Traffic loads must be monitored as the ACLs are removed to ensure that worm traffic from unpatched customers does not have a significant impact on other customers or the provider's backbone. Legitimate customer traffic may also be blocked by the ACLs and support organizations must be notified and prepared to answer customer's questions and complaints.

### 3.3.2 Destination based Black Hole Filtering

Black hole filtering is an effective, quick and simple technique for dropping attack traffic destined toward a victim. Using iBGP as a trigger mechanism, black hole filtering can be remotely triggered across the entire perimeter of a provider's network. This technique is used when more harm is done by the attack filling up a customer's circuit than by the loss of an individual site. Many times, traffic can be redirected to a different IP address through DNS.

Several variations of remotely triggered black hole filtering can be setup. By using different community strings, remote triggers can be setup for different types of routers such as edge and border. Community strings can be setup for different geographic regions or POPs in a provider's network. This flexibility allows the provider to identify the ingress points of the attack and only block traffic at those locations.

### 3.3.3 Attack Distribution and/or Isolation – Anycast

IPv4 anycast implementations have been in use on the Internet for at least the past 10 years. Particularly suited for single response UDP queries, DNS anycast architectures are in use in most tier 1 Internet providers' backbones. Anycast implementations can be used for both DNS authoritative and recursive implementations. Several root name servers are implementing anycast architectures to mitigate DDoS attacks [16]. Black hole filtering is a specialized form of anycast. Sinkholes can use anycast to distribute the load of an attack across many locations [17].

Many DNS anycast implementations are done using eBGP announcements. Anycast networks can be contained in a single AS or spam multiple AS's across the globe. Anycast provides two distinct advantages in regard to DoS/DDoS attacks. In a DoS attack, anycast localizes the effect of the attack. In a DDoS attack, the attack is distributed over a much larger number of servers, distributing the load of the attack and allowing the service to better withstand it.

## 4. Proposed Intrusion Prevention System

Intrusion prevention systems (IPS), also known as intrusion detection and prevention systems (IDPS), are network security appliances that monitor network and/or system activities for malicious activity. The main functions of intrusion prevention systems are to identify malicious activity, log information about said activity, attempt to block/stop activity, and report activity.

The Intrusion Prevention Systems are placed in-line and are able to actively prevent/block intrusions that are detected. More specifically, IPS can take such actions as sending an alarm, dropping the malicious packets, resetting the connection and/or blocking the traffic from the offending IP address. An IPS can also correct Cyclic Redundancy Check (CRC) errors, unfragment packet streams, prevent TCP sequencing issues, and clean up unwanted transport and network layer options.

Intrusion prevention systems can be classified into four different types:

**Network-based intrusion prevention system (NIPS):** monitors the entire network for suspicious traffic by analyzing protocol activity.

**Wireless intrusion prevention systems (WIPS):** monitors a wireless network for suspicious traffic by analyzing wireless networking protocols.

**Network behavior analysis (NBA):** examines network traffic to identify threats that generate DDoS attacks, certain forms of malware, and policy violations.

**Host-based intrusion prevention system (HIPS):** an installed software package which monitors a single host for suspicious activity by analyzing events occurring within that host.

### 4.1 Requirements for Proposed Intrusion Prevention System

The major Functional Requirements for an Intrusion Prevention System need to be discussed before the mechanisms of security architecture. The Functional requirements of an IPS are outlined below:

❖ **Online operations:** In order to perform real time protection, an IPS must operate in online mode at crucial points of the network. IPS can take the required action immediately only when they operate online, discarding any suspicious packets before they reach their target and blocking the remainder flow from that source.

❖ **High performance:** Packet processing must be at the real time traffic speed. Poor performance of IPS will result in slow network speed and lost of packets. Thus, an IPS should perform analysis at very high data rates; degradation in network performance is not at all acceptable.

❖ **Scalability:** An IPS deployment should be scalable in performance and management. IPS could be deployed to medium and large networks without significant performance degradation. NIPS deployment should also provide scalable management for multiple Sensors deployed at choke points of the network.

❖ **Reliability and availability:** Fail of an online device will directly affect the network up-time. Since IPS's are installed on crucial points where any failure can cause the lost of a vital network path and again, can lead to a DDoS condition. Thus, an extremely low failure rate is very important in order to maximize the network up-time and as an assurance, the device should support fail-over to another IPS operating in a fail-over group or provide fail-open option [68]. It is also important that rebooting of online devices will turn into network downtime for the duration of reboot.

❖ **Detection accuracy:** An IPS must detect attacks and should not block the valid traffic flow. Since IPS's operate online, false positives can lead to a DDoS condition and become a new tool for attackers. The user must be able to trust that the IPS is blocking only the malicious traffic [68]. NIPS should not block the valid traffic and prevent employees doing their jobs.

❖ **Ability to perform various types of detection analysis:** IPS's are only as valuable as their detection engines. Success or failure of an IPS depends mainly on its detection engine. There are various detection methods that are used in existing IDS's; each has success at detecting different types of intrusions. Mixing these various methods to use their superior parts and eliminating their weak points can form out a system that is more reliable than any of these methods alone.

❖ **Low latency:** Since IPS is operating online and all traffic has to flow through them, the latency on these devices affects the network performance. Packets should be processed quickly enough that end nodes can not sense the performance degradation. The over all latency of IPS must be as minimal as the latency of other online devices such as firewalls, router, and load balancers.

212

❖ **Easier management:** An IPS allow the security managers to choose the response they want among various response mechanisms. Since IPSs are not only detecting attacks, but also preventing them by limiting or blocking which directly affects the network performance. Thus, configuring an IPS is a complex job. It is important to make the security managers' job of configuration as easy and simple as possible by providing them a user friendly interface to set and change configuration and eliminate the dreadful results of configuration errors [69].

❖ **Safety of historic data:** Beyond detecting and preventing attacks, IPS should save the evidence of an intrusion for historical analysis. In order to do this, historic data could be copied for safe and offline observation. Mechanisms for the safety of these data should be in place.

❖ **Data analysis capability:** IPS should be having a mechanism to allow security managers access individual packets from summary reports, to minimize administration efforts.

❖ **Patch Update:** IPS needs to be updated time to time with patches in order to update with new DDoS attacks, detection and mitigation policies.

❖ **Modular Design:** IPS needs to be made using modular design in order to easily upgrade new functionalities and mechanisms.

### 4.2 Major strengths of proposed intrusion prevention system are:
❖ Automatically Identifies and Blocks Threats
❖ Reduces Time Spent Reviewing Log Files to

**Identify Threats**

- ❖ Reduces Need for Manpower to Monitor Threats
- ❖ Enhances Network Security Architecture

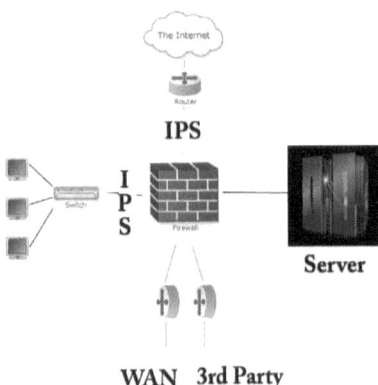

Fig 6: Proposed Intrusion Prevention System

**4.3 Procedure of Proposed Intrusion Prevention**

System [13]

**Step 1:** Client sends a HttpRequest to IPS

**Step 2:** IPS registers the Application Id of Client App

**Step 3:** Then a Random Captcha mechanism starts.

**Step 4:** If Client enters wrong Captcha, the App_Id is recorded and in response a tougher captcha is generated, sensing a DDoS attack.

**Step 5:** At the maximum 3 try has to be given to the Client Application.

**Step 6:** On failure the App Id, Mac Add and IP Add will be blocked.

## 5. Result and Conclusion

Denial of service attacks are a huge threat to the internet as a whole. In order to thwart these attacks over all internet security must be promoted and potential targets must be prepared for the potential attacks. It is critical that security methods evolve with the evolving denial of service attacks to be truly secure. Formal Classification by some community related organization is necessary in the field of Distributed Denial of Service [1].

## References

1. Manish Saxena, Jameel Hashmi, Dr. D.B.Singh, "Classification of DDoS Attacks and their Defence Techniques using Intrusion Prevention System", IJCSCN Volume 2, Issue 5, October-November 2012.
2. *http://www.ijcscn.com/Documents/Volumes/vol2issue5/ijcscn20120205 08.pdf*
3. Howard J., "An Analysis of security incidents on the Internet 1989 – 1995," Carnegie Mellon University, Carnegie Institute of Technology, *<http://www.cert.org/research/JHThesis/Start.html>*, Apr. 1997.
4. Mirkovic J., Martin J. and Reiher P., "A Taxonomy of DDoS Attacks and DDoS defence Mechanisms," UCLA Computer Science Department, Technical report no. 020018.
5. *<http://www.lasr.cs.ucla.edu/ddos/ucla_tech_report_020018.pdf>*, 2002.
6. Spech S. and Lee R., "Taxonomies of Distributed Denial of Service Attacks, Tools and Countermeasures," Princeton University Department
7. of Electrical Engineering, Technical report CE-L2003-004, May 2003.
8. CERT Coordination Center, "Denial of Service Attacks," *<http://www.cert.org/tech_tips/denial_of_ service.html>*, Jun 2001.
9. *http://forum.athena.edu.vn/mang-co-ban-acbn/1521-tim-hieu-kythuat-tan-cong-ddos.html*
10. *http://www.cert.org/tech_tips/denial_of_service. html*
11. Distributed DNS Flooder v0.1b (ddnsf), *<http://www.packetstormsecurity.org/distributed/ddnsf.tar.gz>*, 2001.
12. Flitz, *<http://www.packetstormsecurity.org/distributed/flitz-0.1.tgz>*.

13. Kaiten, <*http://www.packetstormsecurity.org/irc/ kaiten.c*>.
14. Knigth, <*http://www.packetstormsecurity.org/distributed/knight.c*>.
15. Mstream, <*http://www.packetstormsecurity.org/distributed/mstream. txt*>.
16. IPS Sequence Diagram, Manish Saxena,
17. *www.manishsaxena.in/downloads/ips_seq_diag.jpg*
18. Houle K. J. and Weaver G. M., "Trends in Denial of Service Attack Technology," CERT Coordination Center, Oct. 2001.
19. *http://www.cert.org/advisories/CA-1996-21.html*
20. Abley, Joe. "ISC Technical Note Series, Hierarchical Anycast for Global Service Distribution." 2003. Internet Software Consortium, 17Aug. 2003. *http://www.isc.org/tn/isc-tn-2003-1.html*
21. Greene, Barry Raveendran. "Phase 1 – Prepare the Tools and Techniques, Using IP Routing as a Security Tool." ISP Security Bootcamp Singapore 2003. 31 July 2003 <*ftp://ftpeng.cisco.com/cons/isp/security/ISP-Security-Bootcamp-Singapore-2003/H-Preparation-Tools-v3-0.pdf*>. pg. 86-97

# REFERENCES

1.  S. Barlas, A. Earls, M. Fitzgerald, J. Ledford, D. McCafferty, "Mission: Critical", Information Security, September 2004 pg. 26.
2.  "Free Skype internet calls", *www.skype.com*
3.  SKYPE- Wikipedia, *http://en.wikipedia.org/wiki/Skype*
4.  "Internet Security", *http://www.ukessays.com/essays/computer-science /internet-security.php*
5.  A typical Intrusion Detection System, *http://www.cs.bham.ac.uk/ ~mdr/teaching/modules03/security/students/SS1/handout/handout.h tml*
6.  Oliver J., Leahy Dermot M., Tynan J., Mark Smith, Sean G. Doherty, "Firewall technology", Digital Technical Journal, (2), 1997.
7.  NIST Special Publication (SP) 800-61, Computer Security Incident Handling Guide, which is available at *http://csrc.nist.gov /publications/nistpubs/*
8.  "Intrusion Detection FAQ: What is a Honeypot?", *http://www.sans.org /security-resources/idfaq/honeypot3.php*
9.  Prolexic, "Attack report", *http://www.prolexic.com/knowledge-center-ddos-attack-report-2014-q1.html*
10. Johansson, Karsten. "Offensive Operations Model". KSAJ Inc. August 2001. *http://www.penetrationtest.com*
11. ForeScout Technologies, Inc. January 2004. *http://www.forescout.com*
12. Johansson, Karsten. "Offensive Operations Model". KSAJ Inc. August 2001. *http://www.penetrationtest.com*
13. Pfleeger, P. Charles. "Security in Computing". Prentice Hall PTR. Second Edition. p 3. 1997
14. Corum, A. K. Hawaii's Spam Cookbook, ISBN : 0-935848-49-5. Honolulu: Bess Press Inc.
15. G. V. Cormack and T. R. Lynam, "TREC 2005 Spam Track Overview," *http://plg.uwaterloo.ca/~gvcormac/trecspamtrack05, 2005*.
16. Gordon V. Cormack, "Email spam Filtering: A Systematic Review",

17.  ISBN : 978-1-60198-146-2, Volume 1 Issue 4, now Publishers Inc. Hanover, MA, USA

18.  M. Mangalindan, "For bulk E-mailer, pestering millions offers path to profit," Wall Street Journal, November 13, 2002.

19.  Shay, William A. "Firewall". University of Wisconsin-Green Bay. 2000

20.  Yakomba Yavwa. "The Firewall Technology". May 2, 2000

21.  Check Point Software Technologies Ltd. 2000 "Stateful Firewall Technology - Products and Solutions", *http://www.checkpoint.com/ products/technology*

22.  Gómez, Diego González. "Sistemas de Detección de Intrusiones: Capítulo 4". July 2003. *http://www.dggomez.arrakis.es/secinf/ids/ html/cap01.htm*

23.  Espasa Calpe. "Dictionary of the Spanish tongue". 1994

24.  Bace, R. "Intrusion Detection". Macmillan Technical Publishing. 2000

25.  Jupitermedia. "Intrusion Detection System". Last modified: December 13, 2002. *http://www.webopedia.com/tem/I/intrusion_detection _system.html*

26.  Bace, Rebecca and Mell, Peter. "Intrusion Detection Systems". NIST Special Publication. August 2001

27.  Honeypots.net. "Honeypots, Honeynets", 21 November 2003. *http://www.honeypots.org*

28.  Bace, R. a. (August, 2001). Intrusion Detection Systems. NIST Special Publication .

29.  Bace, Rebecca and Mell, Peter. "Intrusion Detection Systems". NIST Special Publication. August 2001

30.  Spitzner, Lance. "Honeypots: Definitions and Value of Honeypots", 29 May, 2003, *http://www.tracking-hackers.com/papers/honeypots.html*

31.  The Honeypot Project, *http://www.honeynet.org/node/157*

32.  Server Firewalls, *http://www.ibm.com/developerworks/library/co-0504_mckegney*

33.  ForeScout Technologies. "Beyond Detection: Neutralizing Attacks Before They Reach the Firewall". Summer 2002

34.  Md. Jameel Hashmi, Manish Saxena and Dr. R. Saini, "Classification of DDoS Attacks and their Defense Techniques using Intrusion Prevention

System", International Journal of Computer Science & Communication N/w, Vol 2(5), 607-614, ISSN:2249-5789

35. CERT Coordination Center, "Denial of Service Attacks," *http://www.cert.org/tech_tips/denial_of_ service.html,* Jun 2001.

36. Blitznet, *http://www.packetstormsecurity.org/ distributed/blitznet. tgz, 1999.*

37. DOSnet.c,*http://www.packetstormsecurity.org/ distributed/DOSnet.c, 2002.*

38. Distributed DNS Flooder v0.1b (ddnsf),

39. *http://www.packetstormsecurity.org/ distributed/ddnsf.tar.gz, 2001.*

40. *Flitz, http://www.packetstormsecurity.org/distributed/flitz-0.1.tgz*

41. *Kaiten, http://www.packetstormsecurity.org/irc/ kaiten.c*

42. *Knigth, http://www.packetstormsecurity.org/ distributed/knight.c*

43. Mstream,*http://www.packetstormsecurity.org/distributed/mstream. txt*

44. Omega v3 Beta,*http://www.packetstormsecurity.org/distributed /omegav3.tgz*

45. Peer-to-peer UDP Distributed Denial of Service (PUD),

46. *http://www.packetstormsecurity.org/distributed/ pud.tgz*

47. Skydancev3.6,*http://www.packetstormsecurity.org/distributed/ skd36 .zip*

48. StacheldrahtV4,*http://www.packetstormsecurity.org/distributed/ stachel.tgz*

49. Tribe Flood Network (TFN), *http://packetstormsecurity.org/groups/ mixter/tfn.tgz*

50. Tribe FloodNet – 2k edition (TFN2k), *http://packetstormsecurity.org/ distributed/tfn2k.tgz*

51. Trin00, http://www.packetstormsecurity.org/ distributed/trinoo.tgz

52. Marchesseau M., ""Trinity" - distributed-denial-of-service attack tool,"

53. *http://www.giac.org/certified_professionals/practicals/gsec/0123.php , 2000.*

54. Dietrich S,. Long N. and Dittrich D., "An analysis of the ``Shaft" distributed denial of service tool," *http://www.packetstormsecurity .org/distributed/ shaft_analysis.txt,* Mar. 2000.

55. Dittrich D., "Analysis of the "Power bot," *http://staff.washington. edu/dittrich/ misc/power.analysis.txt*, 2001.

56. GT Bot (Global Threat), *<http://swatit.org/bots/gtbot.html>*, 2003.

57. D. Moore, "The spread of the code red worm (CRv2),"

58. *http://www.caida.org/analysis/security/codered/coderedv2_analysis. xml.*

59. CERT Coordination Center, "Code Red II," *http://www.cert.org/ incident_notes /IN-2001-09.html*

60. CERT Coordination Center, "Nimda worm," *http://www.cert.org /advisories/ CA-2001-26.html*

61. CERT Coordination Center, "Trends in Denial of Service Attack Technology," October 2001, *http://www.cert.org/archive/pdf/DoS_ trends.pdf*

62. CERT Coordination Center, "erkms and liOn worms," *http://www.cert.org/ incident_notes/IN-2001-03.html*

63. CERT Coordination Center, "Ramen worm," *http://www.cert.org/ incident_notes/IN-2001-01.html*

64. K. Hafner and J. Markoff, Cyberpunk: Outlaws and hackers on the computer frontier, Simon & Schuster, 1991.

65. CERT Coordination Center, "Code Red," *http://www.cert.org /incident_notes/IN-2001-08.html*

66. N. Weaver, "Warhol Worm, "*http://www.cs.berkeley .edu/~nweaver /warhol.html*

67. CERT Coordination Center, "Trends in Denial of Service Attack Technology," October 2001, *http://www.cert.org/archive/pdf/DoS_ trends.pdf*

68. CERT Coordination Center, "DoS using nameservers,"

69. *http://www.cert.org/incident_notes/IN-2000-04.html*

70. CERT Coordination Center, "Smurf attack," *http://www.cert.org/ advisories/ CA-1998-01.html*

71. CERT Coordination Center, "TCP SYN flooding and IP spoofing attacks," *http://www.cert.org/advisories/CA-1996-21.html*

72. D. Dittrich, "The DoS Project's 'trinoo' distributed denial of service attack tool," *http://staff.washington.edu/dittrich/misc/trinoo.analysis*

73. D. Dittrich, "The 'Tribe Flood Network' distributed denial of service attack tool," *http://staff.washington.edu/dittrich/misc/tfn.analysis.txt*

74. D. Dittrich, "The 'Stacheldraht' distributed denial of service attack tool,"*http://staff.washington.edu/dittrich/misc/ tacheldraht.analysis.txt*

75. CERT Coordination Center, "CERT Advisory CA-1999-17 Denial-Of-Service Tools," *http://www.cert.org/advisories/CA-1999-17.html*

76. D. Dittrich, "The 'mstream' distributed denial of service attack tool, "*http://staff.washington.edu/dittrich/misc/ mstream.analysis.txt*

77. S.Dietrich, N. Long and D. Dittrich, "An Analysis of the "Shaft" distributed denial of service tool," *http://www.adelphi.edu/~spock/ shaft_analysis.txt*

78. CERT Coordination Center, " CERT Advisory CA-2001-19 'Code Red' Worm Exploiting Buffer Overflow In IIS Indexing Service DLL," *http://www.cert.org/ advisories/CA-2001-19.html*

79. Steve Martin, B. N. (July, 2005). Analyzing Behavioral Features for Email Classification. Proceeding of: CEAS 2005 - Second Conference on Email and Anti-Spam .

80. Barracuda Networks Predicts Spam Volumes Beyond 95 Percent in 2009. Published in December 2008. *http://www.barracudanetworks. com/ns/news and events/index.php?nid= 322,*

81. Commtouch. Q3 2007 Email Threats Trend Report.

82. *http://www.commtouch.com/downloads/Commtouch2007Q3EmailTh reats.pdf.*

83. Jupitermedia. "Intrusion Detection System". Last modified: December 13, 2002. *http://www.webopedia.com/tem/I/intrusion_detection _system.html*

84. Joe Stewart. Top Spam Botnets Exposed. http://www.secureworks. com/ research /threats/topbotnets, 2008.

85. Kelly Jackson. Srizbi Botnet Sending Over 60 Billion Spams a Day. *http://www.darkreading.com/security/encryption/showArticle.jhtml? articleID=211201479*, May 2008.

86. Kaspersky Lab analyses new version of Kido (Conficker).

87. *http://www.kaspersky.com/news?id=207575791*, April 2009.

88.  Diggy & Glen, "Penguin 2.0 New Google Update: The Facts;*http://www.penguin2.com*",

89.  Red Earth Software, Policy Patrol, "Top 10 spam characteristics", *http://www.policypatrol.com/top-10-spam-characteristics-1-5/* and

90.  *http://www.policypatrol.com/the-top-10-spam-characteristics-6-10/*

91.  *http://www.cisco.com/en/US/tech/tk365/technologies_tech_note 09186a00800a67f5.shtml*

92.  MAC Addressing, *http://standards.ieee.org/develop/regauth/tut/ macgrp.pdf*

93.  Birman, Kenneth. "Reliable Distributed Systems: Technologies, Web Services and Applications". New York: Springer-Verlag, 2005.

94.  *http://www.cert.org/advisories/CA-1996-21.html*

95.  *http://www.cert.org/tech_tips/denial_of_service.html*

96.  Abley, Joe. "ISC Technical Note Series, Hierarchical Anycast for Global Service Distribution." 2003. Internet Software Consortium, 17 Aug. 2003. *http://www.isc.org/tn/isc-tn-2003-1.html*

97.  Greene, Barry Raveendran. "Phase 1 – Prepare the Tools and Techniques, Using IP Routing as a Security Tool." ISP Security Bootcamp Singapore 2003. 31 July 2003 *<ftp://ftp-eng.cisco.com/cons/isp/security/ISP-Security-Bootcamp-Singapore-2003/H-Preparation-Tools-v3-0.pdf>*. pg. 86-97

98.  Abley, Joe. "ISC Technical Note Series, Hierarchical Anycast for Global Service Distribution." 2003. Internet Software Consortium, 17 Aug. 2003. *http://www.isc.org/tn/isc-tn-2003-1.html*

99.  Greene, Barry Raveendran. "Phase 1 – Prepare the Tools and Techniques, Using IP Routing as a Security Tool." ISP Security Bootcamp Singapore 2003. 31 July 2003 *<ftp://ftp-eng.cisco.com/cons/isp/security/ISP-Security-Bootcamp-Singapore-2003/H-Preparation-Tools-v3-0.pdf>*. pg. 86-97

100. Solid Shell Security. *"http://solidshellsecurity.com/tools/synd-syn-deflate-automatic-script-installer.php"*

101. WinPcap, NetGroup, Politecnico di Torino. January 2013. *http://winpcap.polito.it/docs*

102. TCPDump & LibPcap, www.tcpdump.org, January 2013

103. SNORT, *www.snort.org*, January 2013

104. Rehman, Rafeeq Ur. "Intrusion Detection Systems with Snort". Prentice Hall PTR. ISBN 0-13-140733-3. 2003

105. Snort Inline, January 2013, *www.snort-inline.sourceforge.net*

106. IPtables.org , January 2013, *www.iptables.org*

107. Cisco IOS Intrusion Prevention System Deployment Guide, *http://www.cisco.com/en/US/prod/collateral/iosswrel/ps6537/ps6586/ps6634/prod_white_paper0900aecd8062acfb.html*

108. Dell Secure Works, *www.secureworks.com*

109. SANS.org, "Intrusion Detection FAQ: What is a Honeypot?"

110. *http://www.sans.org/security-resources/idfaq/honeypot3.php*

111. Network Associates, "Intrusion Prevention: Myths, Challenges, and Requirements", April 2003. *http://www.networkassociates.com*

112. Top Layer. "Beyond IDS: Essentials of Network Intrusion Prevention". November 2002

113. Microsoft MSDN Library, *"http://msdn.microsoft.com/en-us/library/aa669324%28v=vs.71%29.aspx"*

114. Manish Saxena, Mohd. Jameel Hashmi, Prof. Dr. Dhirendra B. Singh, "Intrusion Prevention System based Defence Techniques to manage DDoS Attacks", The International Journal of Computer Science & Applications (TIJCSA), Vol.(01) No.(08), October, 2012, ISSN:2278-1080

115. Manish Saxena, "IPS Sequence Diagram", *www.manishsaxena.in/downloads/ ips_seq_diag.jpg*

116. Sitepoint, "Easy Spam Prevention Using Hidden Form Fields";

117. *http://www.sitepoint.com/easy-spam-prevention-using-hidden-form-fields/*

118. McCabe, "A Complexity Measure". IEEE Transactions on Software Engineering: 308–320, (December 1976)

119. Manish Saxena, Md. Jameel Hashmi and Dr. Rajesh Saini, "Classification of DDoS Attacks and their Defense Techniques using Intrusion Prevention System", International Journal of Computer Science & Communication N/w, Vol 2(5), 607-614, ISSN:2249-5789

120. Manish Saxena, Mohd. Jameel Hashmi, Prof. Dr. Dhirendra B. Singh, "Intrusion Prevention System based Defence Techniques to manage

DDoS Attacks", The International Journal of Computer Science & Applications (TIJCSA), Vol.(01) No.(08), October, 2012, ISSN:2278-1080

121. Manish Saxena, "IPS Sequence Diagram", *www.manishsaxena.in /downloads/ ips_seq_diag.jpg*

122. Manish Saxena, "Network Intrusion Prevention System Techniques to Manage DDOS Attacks", Universal Journal of Applied Computer Science & Technology, Volume 3, Issue 1, ISSN – 2250- 0987, pg 347, 352.

123. Manish Saxena, Munish Gupta, Vijay Kumar Mishra and Chandra Bhan Singh, "MAS BASED FRAMEWORK FOR NETWORK INTRUSION DETECTION SYSTEM", International Journal of Computer Science & Communication Networks,Vol 2(6), 677-680, ISSN:2249-5789

124. Manish Saxena, Munish Gupta, Prof. Dr. Dhirendra B. Singh, Prof. Dr. Rizwan Beg, "STUDY OF INTEGRATION AND SIMULATION OF VARIOUS INTRUSION DETECTION TECHNIQUES", The International Journal of Computer Science & Applications (TIJCSA), Volume 1, No. 12, February 2013 ISSN – 2278-1080

125. US Patent Publication No. US 2003-0149887, dated August 07, 2003, authored by Satyendra Yadav, titled " Application Specific Network Intrusion Detection

# NEXT GENERATION INTELLIGENT NETWORK INTRUSION PREVENTION SYSTEM

Dr. Manish Saxena

Ph.D. [CS], M.Tech.[CS], M.Phil.[CS], MCA

Rs: 700 /-

NEXT GENERATION INTELLIGENT NETWORK INTRUSION
PREVENTION SYSTEM

**Dr. Manish Saxena**

© **2017 by Research maGma Book Publication**

ISBN - **978-1-387-01579-5**

**Published & Printed By,**
**Research maGma Book Publication**
HON- 14/87, Akkalkot Road, Gandhi Nagar,
Solapur, Maharashtra, India.
**Contact No.** : +91 7385878362
**Website** : http://researchmagma.com
**Email ID:** info@researchmagma.com

# DEDICATION

*"Dedicated to my loving Anu, Ishu, Bruno & Leo."*

## PREFACE

Well, there are thousands of books on Network Intrusion Prevention already flooding the market and libraries. The reader may naturally wonder about the need of writing another book on this topic.

This book is based on my research report which I have written to get degree of Doctorate in Philosophy in Computer Science. This book assumes that you are having basic knowledge of computer science. My objective is not to provide you any catalogue of intrusion prevention protocols, but to come to a behavioral approach to solve this problem of Network Intrusion.

Based on my teaching, industrial and consultancy experience, I have tried to achieve these goals in a simple way. My writing formula was based on:

**Problems + Conceptual Background + Innovative Solution**

I have used simple language so that you can understand the concepts quite easily. I have tried to explain a simple solution to stop spammers and network intruders. The hackers, spammers, crackers and intruders also attend the same college and read the same books. So I believe that only an innovative behavioral approach can solve this problem.

This book will be quite useful for all the levels from undergraduate to research scholars of computer science. Even though multiple readings were done for correcting the errors, but as it is said, "To err is Human" you may find some minor typos in the book. Kindly let me know about your views and provide your valuable suggestions.

Wish you all the best. I am sure you will find this book interesting, innovative and informative.

**Dr. Manish Saxena**

Ph.D.(CSE), M.Tech.(CSE), M.Phil.(CSE), MCA

## ACKNOWLEDGEMENT

At the outset, I am thankful to the Almighty who is most Beneficent and Merciful. It is only with his blessings that I was able to achieve this feat therefore I bow my head in his honour and reverence.

I would take this opportunity to thank my research guides Prof. Usman Ali Khan and Prof. Parvez Mahmood Khan for granting me the privilege of working under their vigil guidance and for their patience during the course of my research work. Their timely advice has given me the right direction thus improving my approach.

I am also thankful to Prof. Ram Pratap Sharma (Director), Prof. Sanjay Srivastava (IQAC Coordinator), Mr. Amit Singh (H.O.D. MCA Dept), Mr. Nupa Ram Chauhan(H.O.D. CSE Dept), Mr. Vijay Kumar Mishra & Mr. Hemant Singh, from FGIET, Raebareli, for their support and help throughout my research work.

I would also like to thank all my friends especially Dr. Alam Sageer, Mr. Rajiv Khandelwal & Mr. Deepak Bharadwaj for providing me their valuable support and encouragement. There are many more who deserve to be thanked whose names I may have forgotten to mention, but their invaluable help, friendship and advice will always be appreciated.

I would also like to thank my beloved wife Mrs. Anisha Saxena for her constant inspiration and support.

I would also like to thank my respected parents Dr. Narendra Mohan and Mrs. Shashi Bala Saxena without whose blessings I would have never reached this position in my life.

**Dr. Manish Saxena**

Ph.D.(CSE), M.Tech.(CSE), M.Phil.(CSE), MCA

# Table of Contents

## Table of Figures

www.ingramcontent.com/pod-product-compliance
Lightning Source LLC
Chambersburg PA
CBHW031834170526
45157CB00001B/302